US SKY SPIES
SINCE WORLD WAR 1

US SKY SPIES
SINCE WORLD WAR 1
MICHAEL O'LEARY

BLANDFORD PRESS
POOLE · NEW YORK · SYDNEY

First Published in the UK 1986 by Blandford Press,
Link House, West Street, Poole, Dorset BH15 1LL

Copyright © 1986. Michael O'Leary

Distributed in the United States by
Sterling Publishing Co., Inc.,
2 Park Avenue, New York, N.Y. 10016

ISBN 0-7137-1555-3
ISBN 0-7137-1692-4 Pbk

Typeset by Poole Typesetting (Wessex) Ltd.
Printed in Great Britain by R. J. Acford, Chichester

British Library Cataloguing in Publication Data

O'Leary, Michael D.
  US sky spies since World War One.—(Blandford
  war photo library)
  1. Reconnaissance aircraft—United States—
  History
  I. Title   II. Series
  623.74' 67' 0973   UG1242.R4

CONTENTS

INTRODUCTION

Few current United States Air Force programs are more sensitive than the manned aircraft reconnaissance mission. Daily, from widely separated bases across the face of the globe, Lockheed SR-71A and TR-1 aircraft launch on missions vital to American and Allied security. These missions are cloaked in a blanket of strict secrecy as aircraft head towards the borders of Warsaw Pact nations, travel to South America, overfly the Middle East or traverse the oceans observing Russian fleet movements. Highly sophisticated, these aircraft are the epitome of aeronautical and electronic development. However, the reconnaissance role was not always so sophisticated.

Although the Great War was basically a static conflict, with bloody fighting throughout an immense system of interconnected trenches, both sides needed some reliable intelligence about each other's movements. The aircraft, which had entered the war in 1914 as a frail contraption, had rapidly developed into an effective fighting machine. Realizing that higher flying aircraft could bring back panoramic photographs of enemy fortifications and movements, each side began modifying aircraft to carry the large cameras of the time. Modifications were very simple. Sometimes a

hole was cut in the bottom of the fuselage through which an observer could point and operate a camera. More often that not, the bulky camera was hefted in the airstream by the observer as he sighted the target area from a rear cockpit. When America entered the War in 1917, its small aircraft industry was not ready to meet the military's demands, so large quantities of foreign aircraft were purchased.

With the conclusion of the Great War and the start of the Roaring Twenties, American airpower was drastically cut back for budgetary reasons. Equipped with just a handful of obsolete aircraft, the Air Service set about establishing the basic framework of an effective air arm with fighter, bomber and observation squadrons—even if there were not enough aircraft to fill the units. The most numerous type of aircraft in Army service was the rather ubiquitous observation machine. The observation aircraft could be almost anything that could carry out the function of 'observing'. These were not specially built aircraft but were usually war veterans with military offensive equipment removed and cameras or observer positions installed in their place. The tough de Havilland DH-4 light bomber fitted quite well into this category.

The first aircraft dedicated to aerial reconnaissance for the American Army Air Corps was the rather ungainly Fairchild F-1A, a civilian Model 71 modified to carry cameras and a photographic crew of three. The F-1A came into service during 1929.

The period between the World Wars was one of little advancement in the gathering of aerial intelligence. The world-wide depression made military funding extremely scarce so the

---

One of the better aircraft used by the Air Service was the French Breguet 14. Powered by a 300 hp Renault, and armed with a single Vickers machine gun firing forward and twin Lewis guns for the observer, the aircraft could carry up to 520 lbs of bombs. Realizing the importance of the photographic mission, selected aircraft were given the dual role, designated by painting 'Photo' on the fuselage, which meant that the aircraft could immediately carry out recon duties. These two American aviators are seen seated in a Breguet 14 which carries the 'photo' designation under the pilot's cockpit.

technology did not advance much. However gathering war clouds in Europe made aerial reconnaissance of prime importance. Just what was Hitler doing? Disguised as 'civil' operations, Sydney Cotton managed to overfly strategic German positions in his Lockheed 12 before the start of hostilities and take important photographs for the British.

It was during World War Two that aerial reconnaissance and intelligence gathering really came into its own. Advanced warplanes were often modified as recon platforms capable of carrying a battery of cameras at high speed and over long distances. Recon flights became a regular part of the war—vital in discovering such items as the V-1 and V-2 launch sites and in planning the D-Day invasion.

After World War Two, the threats imposed by the Cold War and possible Russian aggression called for extremely advanced aircraft and systems. At first, modified bombers like the Boeing B-50 were put to use in the recon mission.

The Soviets quickly developed an advanced defense system against aircraft so the magnificent Lockheed U-2 was born—an aircraft (operated by the Central Intelligence Agency) capable of overflying (at least for a while) Soviet anti-aircraft systems. From experience with the U-2 came the A-12 and the SR-71, aircraft with looks and performance which seem almost unworldly.

Today, the United States maintains the world's largest fleet of intelligence gathering aircraft. The Strategic Air Command operates the Blackbirds, the US Navy guards the free world's oceans with its fleet of Orions, while other dedicated intelligence gathering aircraft monitor Soviet space flights, sniff out Russian radar installations and interfere with communications while other aircraft keep close watch on troubles in developing nations.

This volume can only touch on the vast history of the American aerial intelligence gathering role—offering an overview of the aircraft and the missions undertaken. We have settled on showing just the aircraft used in this mission (apart from the occasional airship!) since the spy satellite program is an entirely separate technology which, by itself, would fill several additional volumes.

The aerial intelligence arena is rapidly changing. The radical SR-71A is being supplemented by even more radical aircraft: the 'stealth' technology aircraft. Several variants of these ultra-secret machines are currently flying but a lid of secrecy is placed on all operations. Stealth was developed to make an aircraft more survivable in today's high-tech anti-aircraft environment. Low radar and infrared signature plus advanced performance will enable the stealth aircraft to continue mankind's most sophisticated intelligence gathering mission. It is difficult to forecast the future, but one can certainly predict the aerial intelligence gathering role will continue with the most advanced aircraft ever built.

Michael O'Leary
Los Angeles, California
June 1985

ACKNOWLEDGEMENTS

The author would like to thank particularly Major William Austen of the USAF, Robert Ferguson of Lockheed – California, and Harry Gann of McDonnell Douglas for their generous assistance.

Abrams: 22. Bell Aerospace: 63(38823), 65(441294). Boeing: 39(P3519). California ANG: 16. Douglas: 5, 27(SM32838), 33, 169(T29911). General Dynamics: 186. Goodyear: 221 (01039-175E). Grumman: 95, 96 (56360), 172 (60307), 174 (777606-1), 175, 214 (764137-15), 215, 220, 224. Hughes: 69-72. H. W. Kulick: 41, 55, 57. W. T. Larkins: 15, 26, 37. Liang/O'Leary Collection: 6, 30, 44, 73, 83, 89, 104, 155, 157, 168, 184. Lockheed: 50 (Y6068), 51 (V7746), 52 (V9492), 53 (V7747), 54 (AD6783), 55 (Z504), 59 (AD39294 & 3293), 60 (P8738), 61 (LA8660), 75 (AD6906), 76 (F833), 77 (AD7229), 79 (AF5378), 81 (H661), 82 (H6099), 92 (CC76), 111 (CC3282), 112 (CC3283), 113, 114 (CC724), 115 (LCA8613), 118 (LA1673), 120 (CC1159), 121 (LA4957), 122 (CC1444), 123 (CC454), 124 (CC1162), 125 (CC1163), 126 (CC1160), 127 (CC1164), 129 (CC1571), 130 (C1063-11), 131 (CC6563-4A), 132 (C645-6569), 133 (CC2622), 134 (CC5388), 135 (CC2405), 136 (CC5798), 137 (CC2906), 138 (CC2904), 139 (CC2903), 140 (CC2137), 141 (CC6090-2), 142 (CC6091-3), 143 (CC6092-36), 144 (CC2166), 145 (CC6091-1), 146 (CC2358), 147 (CC2359), 149, 152, 153 (CC5409-18), 154 (CC2810), 167 (AJ1984), 190 (AG2162), 207 (LAH38A), 208, 212 (CC605), 225 (CC3321). Martin: 103, 183 (P56429). McDonnell Douglas: 85 (HG78-246), 106 (SM303850), 107, 108 (113380), 189 (HG74-106), 191 (SM245511), 192 (HG78-244), 193 (HG82-053C), 222 (C22-000368-003). North American: 80, 86 (9046), 88, 105. Northrop: 74, 223. Northwest Airlines: 40. M. D. O'Leary: 166. Republic: 66-8. Ryan: 17 (3828). Sikorsky: 218, 219. Taylorcraft: 19. R. C. Trimble: 159, UKMOD: 64. W. J. Urbank: 48, 58. USAF: Intro., 4, 14, 18, 21, 23, 24, 28, 29, 49, 62, 78, 84, 87 (37218) 117, 128 (KE70614), 148, 177, 185 (169646), 187 (153461), 194, 196, 197, 199 (175260), 201, 202 (175887), 203, 205, 206 (101452), 209, 226-30. US Army: 8 (17745), 46-7. USCG: 13. US Forest Service: Intro., (W. J. Paeth/162629). US Navy: 10 (1112323), 11, 32 (80-G-19974), 34 (283751), 35, 36, 43, 93, 94, 97, 98, 100 (1060665/D. L. Husman), 101 (Barrett), 102, 109 (1085127), 110, 158 (1117824), 160 (1108736/Stevens), 161 (K112481), 162 (K75465/R. C. Moen), 163 (1181181), 164 (1161180), 165, 170 (1100026/Parkin), 171 (1143765/R. E. Woods), 173 (1164612/C. Christensen), 176 (1133170), 178, 180 (22830/C. C. Curtis), 181, 182 (KN19673/J. L. Edge), 198, 211 (1176185/R. Emmons), 213 (1177122/J. Brown), 216 (K112602/C. Velasquez), 217 (K67085/W. M. Cox). USMC: 42, 210. VFP-61: 156.

1

BLANDFORD WAR PHOTO-FILES

THE INTER-WAR YEARS

1. DH-4s fly a fire patrol over the Olympic National Forest in 1921.

2. Aerial survey and photo reconnaissance was a rugged job during the 1920s. Flying over largely uncharted territory aviators faced extreme high-altitude cold against which these Army aviators – with their DH-4M survey aircraft— are dressed. The great mapping expeditions defined North and South America to a degree previously unknown, but many aircraft and aviators were lost.

3. This photograph of a DH-4 mapping the airmail routes between Los Angeles and Seattle, with Mt Shasta in the background, illustrates the daunting job facing the crews during the 1920s as they flew primitive aircraft over uncharted areas.

1

2

3

4. Martin MB-2 of the 40th Attack Squadron—note the bomb with bat wings insignia. With two 410hp Liberty 12A engines, the wood and fabric MB-2 had a top speed of 98 mph, making the unprotected photographer's position in the bomb aimer / gunner station less than pleasant. A movie camera was very useful during war games for recording 'enemy' troop reactions during simulated attacks.

5. Looking like a giant model, the extremely simple Douglas 0-2 series of observation aircraft proved to be reliable and rugged. An 0-2D (photographed on 14 August 1926) is illustrated, only two of which were purchased, both being improved 0-2Cs. Power came from a 400 hp Liberty. A crew of two was carried.

4

5

6. Fairchild's large, bulky Model 71 monoplane was purchased by the Army as the C-8 light cargo aircraft and the F-1 photographic platform. The XC-8/XF-1 was purchased in 1929 (the XF-1 was the XC-8, s/n 29-325, redesignated) and was followed by eight YF-1s and six production F-1As (all were later redesignated C-8 and C-8A). The F-1 carried three photographers and a pilot. They were powered by a 410 hp Pratt & Whitney R-1340-1 Wasp, and featured folding wings. During World War Two, three 1928 Fairchild FC-2W-2 aircraft (Wasp-powered Model 71 predecessors) were impressed by the military as UC-96s, making them the oldest active photographic aircraft in the Army. The F-1A/C-1A had a top speed of 142 mph, 50-ft span and length of 33 ft.

7. As part of America's 'gun boat diplomacy' in China during the 1930s, observation aircraft were used to spot illegal activities—smuggling, gun running, uprisings—and one of the Navy's most rugged was the Chance Vought O3U Corsair, operated from land bases and catapulted from cruisers. This O3U-1, from USS *Augusta* passes over a Chinese junk during 1935; if hostile, the observer radioed the fleet for an intercept.

6

7

8

8. The ZRS-4 USS *Akron* flying through cloud on 13 June 1932. Construction of the huge, 785-ft long rigid airship began on 7 November 1928 at Akron, Ohio, and was completed on 27 October 1931. The constructor was Goodyear-Zeppelin, a Goodyear Tire & Rubber Company and Luftschiffbau Zeppelin subsidiary. Designed for long-range scouting and reconnaissance, *Akron* and the later *Macon* were unique in having a 60 by 70 ft hangar, for four Curtiss Sparrowhawk scout/fighters. She was powered by eight 560 hp Maybachs. She was lost on the night of 3/4 April 1933, with only three survivors.

9. An imposing photograph of the 'Eyes of the Fleet' *circa* 1924: ZR-1 USS *Shenandoah* moors to USS *Patoka's* mooring mast while a Curtiss H-16 flying boat orbits. Designed by the Bureau of Aeronautics and built at the Naval Aircraft Factory, the 680-ft long ZR-1 was powered by six 300 hp Packard engines and carried 23 crew. She first flew on 4 September 1923. Performance was not what had been predicted since she was inflated with non-explosive helium rather than, as intended, volatile but lighter hydrogen. She was lost on 3 September 1925 in a storm over Ohio.

10. The US Army and the USN each had large observation aircraft fleets during the 1930s, although they clung to the obsolesing biplane configuration. During 1934, the USN adopted the SB (Scout Bomber) designation for two-place carrier aircraft with a dual scouting and dive bombing role. The Vought SBU-1, one of the first with the designation entered in service in 1935; 84 were built.

11. Although it seemed to be a throw-back when ordered into production during 1935, the fabric-covered Curtiss SOC-1 Seagull biplane was built to a specific Navy requirement for the new SO (Scouting Observation) aircraft to be catapulted from USN battleships and cruisers—they could also have landing gear—for long range recon and for spotting for the guns of the big ships. Production ended in 1938 and it was scheduled to be phased out of front line service by 1941, yet, rugged and efficient, it served the entire war. Preparing to take off from a Navy base, this early production SOC-1 has the immaculate pre-war finish and highly polished cowlings.

10

11

12. The USCG wanted a reliable aircraft to extend their patrol range and the five Hall PH-2 all-metal flying boats, ordered in June 1936, filled that task. It gave the USCG an aircraft smaller than the Catalina but bigger than some of the other designs that the Coast Guard was operating. A second order followed in 1939 for seven PH-3s (illustrated) which had an enclosed pilots' cockpit. Although apparently primitive, it was an efficient flying boat that gave the USCG a chance against the U-boats that were coming ever nearer America's coast. The PH-3 had two 750 hp Wright R-1820F-51 radials, a wing span of 72 ft 10 in, length of 51 ft and a top speed of 159 mph.

13. Increasing use of the USCG for coastal patrol led to procuring the rugged, all-metal, twin 450 hp P&W R-985-powered Grumman Goose amphibian, first ordered by the navy as the JRF, a utility transport designation. The JRF-4 could carry two 250-lb bombs or, as here, depth charges underwing. The USCG received ten JRFs which also had provision for survey cameras. It had a top speed of 201 mph.

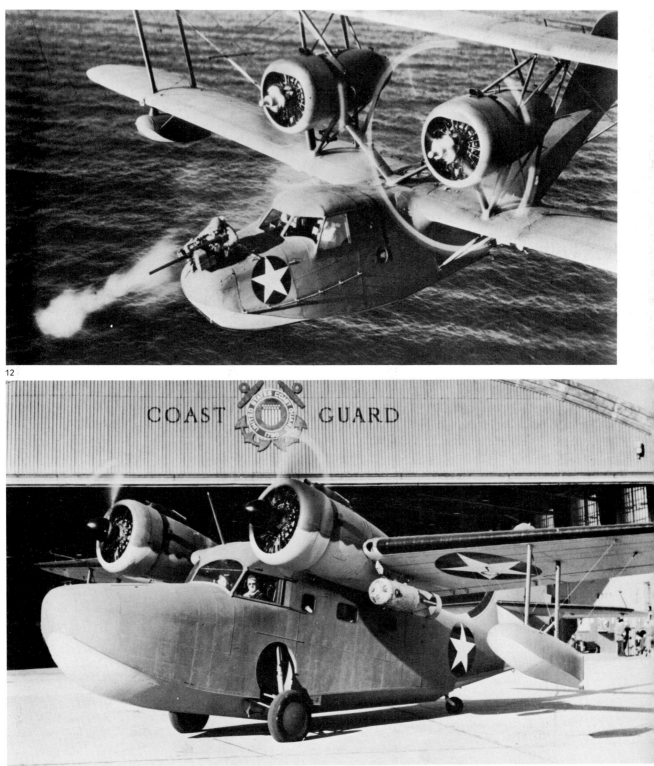

12

13

14. As the 1930s began, much of the Army's budget for its Air Corps went into observation aircraft – during the 1920s and 1930s, Douglas alone built nearly 900. Hundreds of rugged biplanes like the Douglas 0-25A scattered around the country performed a variety of roles and, with few fighters and bombers, pilots at least kept current by flying them. The 0-25A, 50 built, had a geared Curtiss Conqueror 600 hp V-1570-7.

15. The observer/photographer compartment is clearly shown on this California ANG 0-47A. Replacing Douglas 0-38E biplanes, the 0-47s (1,060 hp Wright R-1820-57) were a great improvement in performance and comfort. Some were overseas when Japan attacked. The remainder were relegated to second line duties since they were obsolete. The 0-47A had a 600 mile range, 46 ft 4 in span, 33 ft 7 in length and 221 mph speed.

16. An Olive Drab and Neutral Grey 0-49 115th Observation Squadron, California ANG on manoeuvers at Paso Robles, California. In 1940, Stinson answered the Army's specification for unarmed observation aircraft able to stay in close contact with front-line troops, with the Model 74. Flaps and high lift devices gave good short field performance. Impressed, the Army ordered 142 0-49s, and 182 0-49As in 1941.

14

17. The Ryan XO-51 Dragonfly (s/n 40-703 through 40-705) was built to the same requirement as the YO-50 and O-49 of robust metal construction, the YO-51 had a large slab wing with flaps and slots to achieve extremely low speeds and incredible short field performance. Wide tread landing gear legs allowed rough field operation. The YO-51 was superseded by smaller, lighter Grasshoppers.

18. During the 1930s, the Army wanted observation aircraft with more performance, so a variety of monoplane designs came into being, beginning in 1930 with the all-metal P & W R-1535-7 radial-powered XO-31. Stability and engine installation problems caused considerable redesigning and the first of 90 O-46As was delivered to the Army in May 1936 for ANG units, then modernizing. Although most

were in ANG service, some were serving with the 2nd Observation Squadron, Nichols Field, Luzon, Phillippines, when the Japanese attacked on 8 December 1941—the only Douglas observation monoplanes to see service, albeit very brief. The 101st Observation Squadron O-46A illustrated has the Olive Drab and Grey camouflage that a more warlike AAC was adopting (the white cross was for 1941 war games).

16

17

18

In 1941, the US Army obtained current civil light aircraft to test in the front-line observation/liaison mission. Designated O-57, O-58 and O-59 (L2, L3 and L4 from June 1941) but nicknamed Grasshoppers, all had four-cylinder 65 hp Continentals and could fly low and slow and take-off from and land in very small unimproved areas to drop off photographs or enemy movements reports.

19. Taylorcraft modified the O-57 to meet Army needs. Glazing encompassed the cabin completely, giving excellent vision, and the observer's seat was fully swivelled and adjusted forwards and backwards in flight. Observers had 'walkie-talkie' radios. Missions included short-range reconnaissance, reporting enemy positions, directing artillery, personnel and equipment, transport and troop direction.

20. Fifty O-58s were obtained from Aeronca and further orders followed for the 1941 war games.

21. An L-4 taking-off from a dirt road in North Carolina during the 1941 war games, having delivered vital information to the courier driving the Jeep. The initial batch of 20 O-59s (Piper Cubs) later performed most satisfactorily in the war games. Additional orders followed.

19

20

21

22. The build-up of the West and rapid industrial expansion of major cities proved the usefulness and time / cost-effectiveness of aerial surveying for industrial and suburban planning, but there were no purpose-designed civil aircraft. Abrams Air Craft, Lansing, Michigan, designed an unusually-configured aerial photography and mapping aircraft. After years with Abrams Aerial Survey Corp, the Explorer was stored at NASM.

23. In 1935, the remarkable Martin B-10 entered USAAC service . A clean monoplane, with two 775 hp Wright R-1820-33 radials giving a 213 mph top speed at 10,000 ft, it could outrun most fighters and was also used for high speed photo recon. A 97th Observation Squadron B-10B is seen on 12 July 1939, when most had been withdrawn from front-line service and assigned to units like the 97th.

24. The slipstream wind, high-altitude cold and constant watering of the eyes made moving and sighting large aerial cameras—here, from an 0-47's back cockpit—difficult.

22

23

24

25. As the European war escalated, American readiness slowly improved, as this 1941 photograph of an F-2 shows. The film canister, dropped by parachute from another F-2, will be processed in the portable film laboratory, producing immediate results in the field—a long way from wartime standards, but a start.

26. A military variant of the famous Beech Model 18 civil light transport, the F-2 was the Army's first specialized photo reconnaissance aircraft to be used operationally. Fourteen essentially standard F-2s were purchased in 1940, 13 F-2As were procured in 1943 and 42 F-2Bs during 1944. The F-2 had two 450 hp R-985-19s and 47 ft 8 in span. This 1st Photo Recon Group F-2, in Alaska, during 1941 had orange and green checks.

27. Douglas, attempting to sell more of their successful A-20 Havoc light attack bomber series, responded to an Army request to convert three of the initial order for 63 (ordered in June 1939) into prototypes for photographic reconnaissance aircraft. Trials eventually led to 46 F-3As— A-20Js and A-20Ks modified in 1944, with cameras in the nose and rear bomb bay, and photo flares in the forward bomb bay.

25

26

27

2

BLANDFORD WAR
PHOTO-FILES

WORLD WAR TWO-
US NAVY

28. Considerable numbers of Catalinas were in service at America's entry in to World War Two, and were quickly into action. Searching for U-boats in the Atlantic or Japanese targets of opportunity or searching for downed American aircrews and shipwrecked sailors in the Pacific, they and their crews gave magnificent service. The PBY-5A appeared at the end of 1941 with retractable landing gear and greatly enhanced the usefulness of the rugged aircraft. The Japanese realized the PBY's importance and savagely attacked them, but the PBY-5A carried three .30 caliber and two .50 caliber machine guns and crews scored victories over Zeroes.

29. A USAAF 0A-10A (Army PBY built by Canadian Vickers) swoops low over a down aircrew before alighting to rescue him.

30. PBY-5A Bu No 08098 has been updated with search radar mounted in a large fiber pod behind the cockpit. It bears nine mission 'camera' symbols.

28

31. PBY-5A crew and members of the 6th Combat Camera Unit on Middleburg Island during October 1944 before a photographic mission. Large waist blisters made the Catalina an excellent camera platform. Still cameras are stored in the boxes. The officer on the right carries a movie camera. Rifles and pistols indicate they would be crossing an unfriendly area.

32. The Catalina's value as the 'Eyes of the Fleet' was underscored when this PBY-5A crew spotted a portion of the huge Japanese task force approaching Midway Island on 3 June 1942 and quickly radioed the information back to American forces. 8-V-55 from VP-44 shadowed the force for two and a half hours. The pilot, Ensign Jack Reid, sent a constant flow of information to Midway about the composition, speed and course of the force, constantly varying altitude and course to keep out of sight of any Zero patrols. The battle of Midway was the worst Japanese defeat of the war and a turning point.

30

31

32

33. Graphically illustrating the Navy's 'Eyes of the Fleet' concept of scouting and observation, a Curtiss SOC Seagull biplane observes the effect of the Pacific Fleet's bombardment of Wotje, one of the eight Japanese bases in the Marshall and Gilbert Islands bombarded and bombed on 1 February 1943. The SOC served throughout the entire war, outliving its monoplane replacement.

One of the most famous World War Two observation aircraft was the sturdy Chance Vought OS2U Kingfisher. The initial contract for the first XOS2U-1 was issued on 22 March 1937. Contrasting greatly with the biplanes then in service, the clean all-metal 450 hp P&W R-985–powered monoplane flew for the first time on 20 July 1938 and entered service in August 1940. Its maximum speed was only 164

mph, but it could cruise 805 miles, radioing information back to the Fleet and earning its title 'Eyes of the Fleet'. A total of 1006 was built. The Naval Aircraft Factory also built the type, designated OS2N-1. Production ended in 1942, but they served actively until VJ-Day.

33

34

35

34. As landing craft approach and larger ships fire their guns, this Vought OS2U Kingfisher circles above a Pacific atoll, the observer radioing back vital information to the Fleet.

35. The OS2U could be fitted with either land or, as here, float gear when it could be catapulted from cruisers and battleships.

36. Some Kingfisher crews were decorated for valor, snatching airmen from Japanese occupied harbors while under heavy fire. This unusually-camouflaged Kingfisher found this group of survivors but could not accommodate them all. With some on the wing and the rafts tied to the floats, the pilot taxied across the ocean until reaching friendly ships. (USN)

37. The SBD-1P, 2P, 3P and 4P were photo recon conversions of the successful Douglas SBD Dauntless dive-bomber. After the War's end, the Dauntless was rapidly phased out of active service but a few were retained as hacks or as photographic platforms like this unusual natural-metal Dauntless, over San Francisco bay, assigned to the Naval Air Transport Service.

36

38. The single-seat Curtiss SC Seahawk, last of the battleship/cruiser catapult observation aircraft, was designed to a US Navy specification issued in mid-1942. The XCS-1 (Wright R-1820-62) first flew on 16 February 1944. Production aircraft deliveries, totalling 500, began during October 1944. It saw service in the Pacific. Postwar, surviving SCs were quickly scrapped.

39. The Boeing XPBB-1 Sea Ranger has the distinction of being the largest twin-engine flying boat built in the United States. Powered by two R-3350-8 Cyclones, it spanned 139 ft 8 in, was 94 ft 9 in long, and had a maximum weight of 101,130 lb. After a single prototype had been built, and flown on 5 July 1942, the Navy cancelled it. Its wing was used for the B-29.

40. The B-24 Liberator's spacious fuselage made an ideal basis for a camera platform. In 1943, the designation F-7 was assigned to a B-24D converted by Northwest Airlines, St Paul, Minnesota. Operational F-7s were modified from B-24Hs and 86 F-7As (illustrated) from B-24Js, which also provided the basis for the F-7B. Most operational use was in the South Pacific.

38

39

40

41. 42. Large working spaces in the new B-17 and B-24 bombers made the aerial photographers' task easier, shown by cameramen in a B-24 **(41)** and USMC PB4Y-1 Liberator. Aerial photography was crucial in America's Pacific island war, each Japanese-held island being completely photo-mapped before an attack, using infrared and color (still fairly rare) to define camouflaged targets.

43. PROJECT CADILLAC was set up by MIT (Massachusetts Institute of Technology) and the US Government to conduct a program that would lead to some form of radar early warning. Various types of early radar units were tested from atop Mount Cadillac in Maine. MIT concluded that radar could be carried by an aircraft to give early warning of approaching ships and aircraft. CADILLAC I led to airborne early warning radar being installed in an Eastern TBM-3 Avenger, normally a carrier-borne torpedo bomber, offering a fair amount of internal space and good lifting capabilities. A General Electric AN/APS-20 was installed in a bloated fiber radome, replacing the bomb bay. Designated TBM-3W, it became the first airborne early warning aircraft.

41

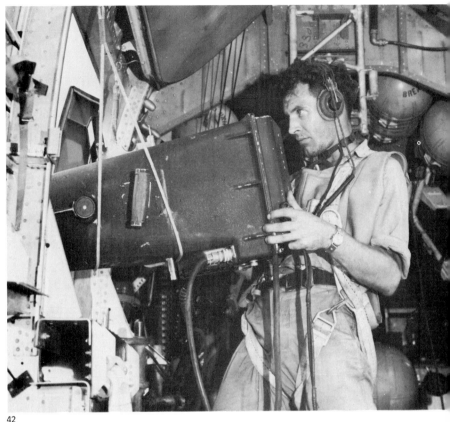

42

44. The TBM-3W and -3W2 soldiered on with the Naval Air Reserve well into the 1950s, but their equipment, in a few short years, had become more than obsolete. During the war, the AEW Avengers were sometimes able to detect incoming *kamikaze* attacks, letting the carriers scramble fighters. CADILLAC I produced a workable system but MIT realised that a larger more efficient airframe was needed.

45. Under PROJECT CADALLAC II, the Navy equipped around 32 B-17Gs redesignated PB-1Ws, as Combat Information Centers (CIC), developed to counter the *kamikaze* threat. AN/APS-20B search radar was installed in the large belly radome with operators and screens in the spacious fuselage. The radar had a limited fighter direction capability with a range of 65 miles against low-flying aircraft and 200 miles against shipping.

PB-1Ws served with units such as VPB-101, VC-11, VP-51, VW-1 and VW-2. Most had no turrets but this natural-metal example retains all except the belly installation. They had provision for underwing fuel tanks.

44

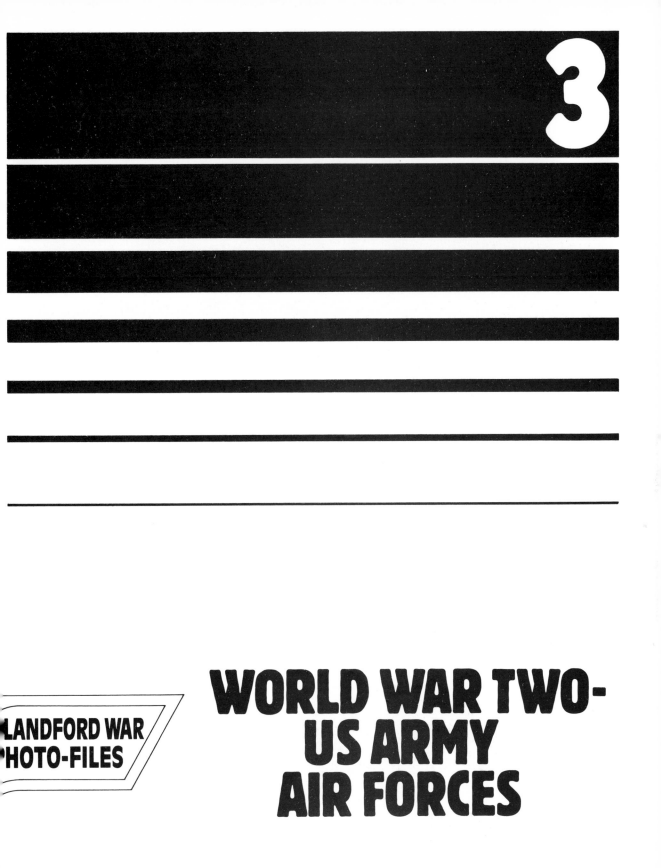

3

BLANDFORD WAR
PHOTO-FILES

WORLD WAR TWO-
US ARMY
AIR FORCES

46. Though the Army operated several types of 'Grasshopper' during World War Two, the Piper L-4 Cub came to represent the light liaison/observation role, and was produced in the greatest numbers—5553. Simple handling characteristics and low maintenance requirements made it very popular in the field. Here, a flight passes in review with motorized units at Fort Sam Houston in April 1942.

47. Its 'mighty' 65 hp Continental four-cylinder engine ticking over, an L-4B prepares for a reconnaissance mission. The pilot has moved his seat all the way forward while the observer has scrunched around in the rear, tilted up the side window and uses the folding door as a prop for the large hand-held aerial camera. Such uncomfortable seating was typical of the Grasshopper missions. This Olive Drab/Neutral Grey L-4, *Thunderbird*, has red-outlined national insignia, officially in use only for Operation TORCH, when L-4s flew their first combat missions, off USS *Ranger*, observing for the Allied North African invasion.

46

47

48. The insignia on this L-4 suggests that the 8th Photo Squadron had traded in their Lightnings. However, found wrecked by the 8th while stationed on Dulag, Leyte, enlisted personnel rebuilt it. It was used for courier flights and R&R hotdogging by pilots and enlisted men. When the 8th moved to Okinawa, it was tied down to the deck of an LST. During rough weather, two jeeps broke loose and crushed it.

49. The Stinson L-5 Sentinel, a military adaptation of the civil 105 Voyager, was initially procured under the designation O-62 in 1942. Over 3000 were constructed—the second most numerous liaison aircraft. Used for everything from scouting to observation to photography to ambulance aircraft, it served on all fronts but in particularly large numbers in the Pacific Theater. It had a 185 hp Lycoming 0-435-1, 34-ft span, a length of 24 ft 1 in and 130 mph top speed. This L-5A is surrounded by Sea Bees on a Pacific air strip under construction.

48

49

50. As the Army's need for high speed photo reconnaissance aircraft grew, several production fighters were studied for modification. The Lockheed P-38 Lightning was ideal—fast at high altitude, its unique configuration offered a distinct advantage since the large central pod could carry cameras instead of guns without obstructing the large lenses' field of view. Lockheed modified P-38Es on the production line to F-4-1-LOs (Model 222-62-13). It had 1150 hp Allison V-1710-21/29 engines. Quickly pressed into service, F-4s went into action in November 1942 with the 5th Photo Reconnaissance Squadron in North Africa.

51. The most common fighter converted to the photo recon role. Over 1400 F-4s and F-5s were accepted by the Army. Lockheed's Burbank flight line has an F-5B-1-LO in the foreground with F-4As and F-5Bs in the background. The F-5B-1-LO (Model 422-81-21), based on the P-38J-5-LO, had the F-5A-LO nose camera package (five cameras instead of the four carried by the earlier F-4s), and Allison V-1710-89/-91 engines; 200 F-5B-1-LOs were built. Removeable flaps over the camera ports protected the thick glass. The lead aircraft is in the unusual 'haze' high-altitude camouflage

50

51

52

scheme, produced by spraying with layers of different paint, mottling shadow areas and the sides. Very difficult to apply, aircraft from the factory had individual interpretations. Lockheed produced an easier scheme using synthetic haze paint, a Sky Blue base followed by Flight Blue in shadow areas and along the sides, a very subtle scheme that appeared to be one overall color.

52. F-5B-1-LO 42-67332 in synthetic haze paint on a test flight from the Burbank factory.

53. Topping-off a synthetic haze-camouflaged F-5B for delivery, its camera ports covered for the delivery flight. The nose-shape of early photo Lightnings resembled the fighter's, giving an extra 'edge' as the enemy would not pursue them so readily.

54. Perhaps the least attractive Lightning photo bird was the F-5G-6-LO. Based on the P-38L-5-LO airframe, it was modified at Lockheed's Dallas facility with a larger, longer nose for more camera and film gear. Their two Allison V-1710-111/113 engines produced a war emergency rating of 1600 hp at 28,700 ft. The first F-5G, s/n 44-25067, runs up on the Dallas ramp.

53

55. The nose of a P-38 modified to F-4 configuration (faired-over gun ports are visible on the original print), showing one oblique and two vertical camera positions. The F-4 nose could carry four cameras, the pilot operating their controls via switch boxes. The first F-4s were retained for training, designated RF-4-1-LO, R indicating restricted (non-combat) use.

56. A pilot assists a crewman in installing a film pack in his standard Army Olive Drab and Neutral Grey F-5A. The camera bay's large upward opening doors afforded excellent access. Equipped with five cameras, seven ports gave excellent coverage. F-5s could penetrate enemy areas at either high or low altitude, usually at full power since speed was the key to survival for the pilots.

57. A USAAF camera technician prepares to place a film pack in the camera compartment of F-5A-10-LO s/n 42-13079, which has an early variation of haze camouflage. Based on the P-38G, 40 F-5A-10-LOs were built. In Britain, the Ninth Air Force operated four photo recon squadrons (30th, 31st, 33rd and 34th) from early 1944, which moved to the Continent following the invasion.

55

56

57

58. World War Two photo recon pilots did not have an easy job, especially when in areas heavily protected by fighters. Never receiving the publicity of fighter pilots, photo recon groups became rather clannish. These 8th Photo Squadron pilots at Dulag, Leyte, during spring 1945 pose in the officers' club they built as a gathering place in their hostile environment.

59. An interesting modification apparently undertaken in the field to enable a standard P-38 fighter to record the results of strafing. One of the nose-mounted .50 caliber machine guns has been replaced by a movie camera under a handmade blister, the aluminum strip being removed prior to flight to give a relatively clear field of view. The photographs were taken on 14 May 1945.

60. The large nose section on the first F-5G-6-LO (a converted P-38L-5-LO), showing the ADF 'football' antenna added after initial testing. The serial number's last four digits have been repeated on the nose; the '1' denotes that it is the first F-5G. It had a port in the extreme nose, oblique ports and a large vertical port.

58

59

60

61. A photograph taken on 25 June 1944 at 13,000 ft over Occupied France by an F-5 with an F-24 camera mounted vertically, showing a formation of US Eighth Air Force B-17Gs heading towards a target at low altitude—a high altitude bomber and it is interesting to see the Fort down low, vulnerable to anti-aircraft fire. Very fine grain photo recon film allowed portions of the negative to be enlarged many times.

62. It did not take the US Army Air Forces long to realize that one of the best performing British aircraft of World War Two was the de Havilland Mosquito, reverse Lend-Lease acquisition of Mosquito PR MK xv1s taking place after the Eighth Air Force established itself in Britain. For weather observation and to check targets before and after bomber strikes, like NS569 illustrated, they were greatly appreciated for their ability to

outrun some enemy fighters. Most USAAF recon Mosquitos served with the 25 Bombardment Group (Reconnaissance) at Watton. Some were used to drop agents and supplies into Occupied Europe. Most American PR MK xv1s were overall Photo Recon Blue with crimson tail sections.

61

62

63. To assist British aircraft production, the Mosquito was produced in Canada. By late 1942, they were coming off the de Havilland of Canada Ltd line at Toronto heavily financed with American funds. The Canadians built 1034. The USAAF acquired 40 (s/n 43-34924—63) F-8s, essentially a Packard Merlin-powered, B Mk xx with photo recon modifications.

64. An RAF technician installing cameras into a PR Mosquito similar to the type used by the Eighth Air Force. Some American Mosquitos were equipped with 12 M46 700,000 candlepower photoflashes in the bomb bay to throw details on the ground into sharp relief at night.

65. Bell Aircraft became responsible for maintaining and modifying USAAF F-8s, here at a Bell facility alongside Beech AT-11 Kansan trainers, being prepared for entry into active service since work on the ariframes is minimal. Note the under wing slipper tanks. (Bell Aerospace/441294)

63

64

65

Possibly the most graceful of all large reconnaissance aircraft, and the ultimate embodiment of piston-engine streamlining, the Republic XF-12 (later redesignated XR-12) Rainbow was built to an exacting 1943 USAAF requirement drawn up by the USAAF's Photographic Section of the Air Technical Service from recommendations made by Colonel Elliot Roosevelt, calling for a very long range, high speed aircraft especially constructed for the USAAF's reconnaissance mission. Republic's chief designer, Alexander Kartveli, felt that to achieve the required altitude and speed— over 40,000 feet and over 400 mph—four large piston engines would be required. Picking the largest available, the 3,500 hp R-4360, he and his design team created a machine with the absolute minimum of drag. The USAAF awarded Republic contract W3308 AC2135 in March 1944 for the construction of two prototypes at a cost of $6,545,699 (including some spares). Typical of so many wartime aircraft, design and construction of the Rainbow were rapid rate.

66. 67. The first prototype, s/n 44-91002, rolled out of the factory during December 1945, and first flew on 4 February 1946 with Lowry

66

67

Brabham as pilot, Oscar Hass as co-pilot, and James Creamer as flight engineer. It was intended entirely for flight test, and none of the sophisticated photo reconnaissance equipment was installed. After extensive testing, it was used as an artillery target at Aberdeen Proving Ground. As the war had ended, flight testing was less than urgent, the entire program for building new aircraft slowing almost to a standstill.

68. The second Rainbow, s/n 44-19003, did not fly until 12 August 1947. It was the first true photographic plane since it carried many cameras including a complete dark room to process film in flight; three camera compartments housed any sort of camera combo possible. It met an unpleasant end during a test flight on 4 November 1948 when the number two engine exploded. Flight testing on the two prototypes was extended to draw out the program. Pan American Airlines were interested in the Rainbow as a high speed transatlantic passenger ship, but after the military cancelled its initial order for 20, Republic could not produce an affordable airliner. Flying characteristics were superior. The first four-engine aircraft to fly at Mach .8, its elegant 129-ft wing gave excellent high-altitude performance.

69. Howard Hughes in the second prototype Hughes XF-11 on 5 April 1947. Built to the same specification as the Rainbow, Hughes' answer to the problem of high-speed, high-altitude photo reconnaissance, the ultra sleek XF-11 was the product of Hughes' fascination with long-range aircraft. The earlier, highly secret, privately-funded Hughes D-2 high-speed long-range bomber, constructed from Duramold—a plastic impregnated wood product—was first flown on 20 June 1943 but disappointing performance led to redesigns that resulted in the XF-11. Hughes demanded absolute attention to detail on the prototype XF-11s. Every rivet was flush, every joint smoothed, filled and sanded to give as streamlined a shape as possible. Airframes were painted overall Light Grey (16473), then oversprayed with an extremely shiny nylon-based clear top coat which, when dried and cured, was heavily waxed and polished. The XF-11 spanned 101 ft 5 in, and had an overall length of 65 ft 5 in, a ceiling over 40,000 ft (the center pod was completely pressurized), and a speed over 400 mph. The second prototype (s/n 44-76156) had P&W R-4360-37s *without* contra-rotating propellers. The first prototype, s/n 44-70155, had R-4360-31 engines with contra-rotating

propellers. On an early test flight on 7 July 1946, the right rear propeller failed and went into reverse, causing the XF-11 to descend rapidly in a spiral. It crashed into Beverly Hills and exploded. Badly injured, Hughes dragged himself from the wreckage. The hospital listed his chances of survival as slim but did not count on Hughes' will.

70. 71. More or less recovered from his crash, Hughes first flew the second prototype from his private airport at Culver City, California, on 5 April 1947.

72. The nose carried an impressive camera array firing through various ports, and doors in the rear left boom could be opened in flight to expose four cameras. It carried a pilot and navigator / photographer / back-up pilot.

70

71

72

73. One of the most effective photo recon aircraft of World War Two was the F-6 variant of the P-51 almost all versions of which were modified. Unlike P-38 conversions, the armament was retained – useful over Occupied Europe. This F-6D-30-NT, s/n 45-11670, is seen post-war at Mines Field, Los Angeles (its photograph ports are on the left).

74. The post-war military economy did not offer the Northrop F-15A Reporter a large role and only 36 were built and delivered during 1946. The F-15A was an excellent performing aircraft and handled much like the fighter from which it was derived—its top speed being higher than the P-61. Cameras were mounted in positions in the extreme nose, offering a wide field of view. The aircraft spanned 66ft and was 49 ft 7 in long. As the test pilots climb out of the first Reporter, the large paddle blade Curtiss-Electric propellers of the up-rated P & W R-2800-Cs are shown to advantage, the design offering excellent high-altitude 'bite' in the thin air.

73

74

4

BLANDFORD WAR
PHOTO-FILES

KOREA AND THE COLD WAR - US AIR FORCE

75. One derivation of the basic P-80 airframe was the XF-14-LO, s/n 44-83024. This machine, a YP-80A-LO, was converted to have a modified nose that would carry cameras instead of six .50 caliber machine guns. The success of the concept led to orders for the F-14-10 (designated RF-80A after June 1948), basically a stock P-80 with a new nose for camera gear including K-17 and K-22 cameras. The aircraft in the photograph, s/n 44-84998, was a P-80A-1-LO that was modified as an F-14A development aircraft; 38 P-80A-5-LOs were converted to F-14As, and 114 built new.

76. This massive 40-inch camera could shoot through a port below the F-14A's nose, adjustable racks being provided for different cameras. Early P-80s were finished very precisely to increase speed, the airframe was covered with body putty, then sanded very smooth and sprayed with a grey enamel which was baked in a special oven. It rapidly chipped and cracked and was soon replaced by natural aluminum finish.

75

76

77

77. The F-14A's nose hinged forward for access. In 1953, 98 F-14As were overhauled and their original 3850 lb thrust General Electric J33-GE-11s were replaced by new 5400 lb thrust Allison J33-A-35 turbojets.

78. Camera options available to an RF-80C of the 67th Tactical Reconnaissance Wing based at Taegu Air Base (K-2) during 1951.

79. An RF-80A being prepared for a mission in extremely foul weather. During the severe Korean winter, RF-80s recorded North Korean and Chinese movements, the recon photos giving the Allies pin-point target locations, ensuring—once they had the upper hand—that attacks continued on almost a 24-hour basis. The canvas wing covers prevent ice buildup.

80. Small cameras record the 98 photo missions of RF-80A-5-LO s/n 45-8373 *Darlin' Doris* of the 15th Tactical Reconnaissance Squadron. Standing orders stated that RF-80 pilots were to turn back and head home at the first sight of MiGs-15s, missions only being continued if the target was of vital importance and if heavy air cover was provided by F-86 Sabres.

78 79 80

81. FP-80A-LO (an interim designation between F-14A and RF-80A) s/n 44-85483, on a test flight from the Burbank factory, with the dive brake deployed in order to formate with the photo plane. It has large buzz numbers on the rather ungainly photo nose. By this point in production the baked-on grey finish had been replaced by bare metal.

82 During the late 1940s and the early 1950s, airframe manufacturers frantically converted experimental and production aircraft to 'specialized' photo reconnaissance variants. Lockheed offered the RF-90A version of their XF-90. The XF-90 first flew on 6 June 1949. A long range bomber escort with two Westinghouse J-34s, six 20 mm cannons and proposed range of 1600 miles, it was in competition with the XF-88A and YF-93A, and Lockheed was hedging its bet with the RF-90A. This elaborate molded plexiglass mockup showed the proposed installation, including a motion camera in the tip. The penetration fighter program was dropped when the Korean War started, and the XF-90A and RF-90A died.

81

82

83. The Republic RF-84F Thunderflash, one of the more numerous 1950s USAF photo recon types, was an F-84F Thunderstreak development, the J65-W-1 turbojet's nose intake being replaced by a camera bay and four 0.5-inch guns, and wing root intakes. First flown in February 1952, production, totalling 718, began that year. It served with the SAC, TAC and several NATO air forces, a *Luftwaffe* RF-84F being shown.

84. During the early 1950s, the USAF made many 'one-off' modifications using surplus World War Two aircraft and including the conversion of this North American B-25 Mitchell's nose to house camera, possibly television, equipment.

85. The military realized that the fast P & W R-2800–powered Douglas A-26 Invader would make an excellent high speed recon platform, carrying cameras in its large bomb bay, nose and rear fuselage. A few A-26Cs were modified to FA-26C configuration (B-26C and RB-26C from June 1948). Their main mission was night recon, and RB-26Cs, usually overall Black, saw considerable action in Korea, using flares to light up targets. Some also carried radar and ECM equipment. (Mc Donnell Douglas / HG78-246)

83

84

85

86. North American, reasoning that a good fighter would make a good photo recon bird, converted F-100A s/n 53-1551—here, seen on 28 February 1955—to an RF-100A. The four 20 mm cannons were removed from the lower fuselage which was built up and expanded downwards to carry cameras while the cockpit was fitted with associated controls and instruments. The neat modification only slightly impaired normal performance but the USAF did not produce the RF-100A, which quietly disappeared.

87. As the huge six-piston-engined Convair B-36 (later augmented with four podded jets) was capable of impressive speeds, altitudes and range while carrying a large load, many were modified during construction to RB-36 configuration, carrying 18 crew, 14 cameras, 80 flash bombs and extra ECM equipment, plus 16 guns in retractable turrets, except the tail gun. Variants included the RB-36D (24 built), RB-36E (22 converted from B-36As and the YB-36), RB-36F (24 built), and RB-36H (973 built, capable of carrying 1400 lb of chaff).

86

87

89

88. In 1947, the North American B-45 Tornado was selected as America's first jet bomber. Several variants quickly followed, including the photo recon RB-45C, ordered on 11 November 1947. First flying on 3 May 1949, the order for 33 was completed during 1950. The RB-45C had four General Electric J47-GE-13s of 5200 lb dry static thrust, 5820 lb with water injection.

89. In view of the RB-45C's high top speed, 509 mph at 32,500 ft, armament was limited to two .50 caliber machine guns in a tail turret, but the MiG-15 rendered it quickly obsolete for sorties over well-defended areas in Korea. It switched to clandestine operations, regularly penetrating Soviet and Chinese airspace from bases in Britain, Europe and Turkey, several disappearing during these flights. A detachment assigned to the RAF carried out clandestine missions in conjunction with the USAF. Cameras were contained in four compartments: four in a vertical station in the rear fuselage; four at the split vertical station; one forward oblique camera; and a trimetrogon K-17C. The bomb bay carried 25 M-122 photo flash bombs and additional fuel tanks.

88

90. An RB-50B crew stands in front of their aircraft, with some of the cameras and special equipment for a lengthy recon flight in front of them. All but one of the 45 B-50s built were converted into the R (reconnaissance) role. By 1951, 14 had become RB-50Es, 14 became RB-50Fs with SHORAN, and 15 RB-50Gs with extra radar and recon equipment.

91. As the Cold War warmed up aerial reconnaissance became even more important. Here, a Boeing RB-50 crew undergo a lengthy briefing prior to a recon flight. Such missions were long and grueling—pencilled in on the mission board is eight plus hours while the map indicates that an overflight of Cuba was included.

92. One of the least-known sky spies, five Lockheed RB69A were built for the USAF by Lockheed (s/n 54-4037—'41) while two P2V-7s were later converted (s/n 54-4042 and '43). Supposedly for an EWf (Electronic Warfare) 'training' progam, the Neptunes, loaded with secret SLAR and ELINT gear, were in fact flying clandestine missions near and sometimes over Russian and Chinese borders.

90

91

92

5

KOREA AND THE COLD WAR - US NAVY

93. Sixty photo recon Grumman F8F-2P Bearcats were built during 1948-49, with camera installations in the fuselage, but retaining two of the four 20mm cannon. Assigned to VC-61 (later becoming VP-61), one of the Navy's top recon units, the F8F-2P was very soon replaced by more advanced jets. BuNo 121583 crashed into the crash barrier during carrier qualifications aboard the USS *Valley Forge* on 19 July 1949.

94. During the 1940s and 1950s, US Navy airships carried out an important, but rarely publicized reconnaissance mission. The ZPG-1 series prototype delivered in 1954 had a volume of 875,000 cu ft and a length of 324 ft. Powered by two 800 hp Wright radials, it was capable of carrying a 14-man crew in a double-deck car. The type evolved into the ZPG-3W (four built) with volume increased to 1,516,000 cu ft and length to

403 ft, and powered by 1525 hp Wright R-1820-88s. Carrying a large search radar inside the envelope, the ZPG-3Ws were used as AEW platforms, but the fatal crash of one in June 1960 spelled the end of the Navy's airship program. The others were withdrawn from service on 28 June 1961.

93

94

95

95. During the 1940s and 1950s, the US Navy developed the Hunter/Killer method of dealing with enemy submarines and some surface targets. Originally using modified Avengers, one carrying detection equipment, the other the weapons, the concept was refined by Grumman with the XTB3F-1, a fast torpedo bomber that had a P&W R-2800 in the nose and a small Westinghouse 19XB-2B turbojet in the tail. The torpedo bomber concept was quickly dropped but the large aircraft was developed into the XTB3F-1S (sub hunter) and the NTB3F-2S (sub killer) — both minus the jet. They had good load-carrying capability and performance. Production began in 1950 with the aircraft redesignated AF-2W (153 built), with AN/APS-20 search radar mounted in a pod under the fuselage, and AF-2S (193 built), which had a spacious weapons bay, a searchlight under the left wing and a short-range AN/APS-31 radar pod under the right wing. Each carried two crew members in the cockpit while the AF-2W had two radar operators in the fuselage. The Guardian came to be regarded as the first practical AEW aircraft although the use of two machines was a bit difficult in actual combat situations.

96. The Grumman F9F-2/5 Panther was developed into the swept-wing F9F-6/8 Cougar, with an up-rated 7250 lb st thrust J48-P-8 and more advanced systems, which first flew on 20 September 1951. As with the Panther they were modified into photo recon platforms as F9F-6Ps (60 built) and F9F-8Ps (110 built) with large, angular noses housing cameras and ports ; not fast, they needed fighter protection.

97. The McDonnell F2H-2P Banshee (88 built) was yet another Navy development to adapt a standard carrier fighter to the photo recon role: BuNo 128885 of VC-61 flies near Mt Fujiyama, Japan, on 9 November 1953. Powered by two 3150 lb st thrust Westinghouse J34-WE-34 turbojets, it had a top speed of 575 mph and range of 1100 miles, and, unarmed, carried six cameras in a modified nose.

98. Lt Commander H. A. Tompkins from VC-61's detachment ABLE overflying home base (USS *Boxer*) in F9F-2P BuNo 123706 on 10 September 1951. The US Navy's first really practical carrier-based jet fighter was the PBW J42-P-6–powered Grumman F9F Panther. It was not long before an unarmed photo recon version was built, with cameras, mounts and ports in the nose. The F9F-2P was very valuable during the Korean War.

96

97

98

99. Not surprisingly, the USAF and USN used the Douglas C-47 Skytrain/Dakota — the 'Gooney Bird' — for EW and special reconnaissance roles. In Vietnam, EC-47M, N and P variants were used for electronic reconnaissance, AEW and other clandestine missions. The R4D-5Q illustrated, BuNo 17173, was used as an Electronic Warfare training platform at NAS Los Alamitos where it was stationed with the local Naval Air Reserve.

100. The last of the USN's glorious flying boats, the Martin P5M Marlin developed from the World War Two Mariner. The prototype XP5M-1 flew on 30 May 1948. The huge boat spanned 118 ft 2 in, had a length of 100 ft 7 in and had a top speed of 251 mph courtesy of two 3450 hp Wright R-3350-32WAs. The first production model flew on 22 June 1951; 114 P5M-1s were built. The P5M-2 (145 built) was a major redesign with improved hull, T-tail and improved interior. The first flew on 23 June 1954. Production continued until 1960. Designed for long range patrol duties, it was well armed with a crew of 11 and had radar, AN/ASQ-8 MAD and other search equipment plus cameras. Redesignated P-5 in the early 1960s, during the last portion of its career they patrolled the coast of Vietnam; the P5M-2 illustrated, on 18 May 1962, was assigned to VP-45.

99

101. Two P-5s replenish supplies from the USS *Curritcuk* during military manoeuvers off Santa Catalina, California, on 15 June 1963. Many P-5s called San Diego's North Island NAS home when they were not on patrol. Ten P5M-2s were built for France's *Aéronavale* and were used for patrol duties.

102. The elegant Martin P6M-1 Seamaster was the Navy's first, and last, attempt at producing a jet-powered flying boat patrol aircraft. Powered by four 10,000 lb thrust Allison J71 turbojets, the XP6M-1 flew for the first time on 14 July 1955. A rotary bomb bay carried bombs, mines or a large photo recon pod. When closed, the door would self-seal and become watertight. Two XP5M-1s were built but both were destroyed in testing.

Six YP5M-1s followed, along with four P5M-2s, and these were powered with 15,000 lb thrust P&W J75-P-2s. Developmental problems plagued the program. The Navy abandoned its patrol flying boat program and decided to concentrate on land planes in the long-range patrol role. (USN)

103. As World War Two drew to an end, the US Navy was fascinated with the concept of combining large piston engine radials with jet power. Several of these designs actually got off the drawing board, including Martin's very large P4M Mercator. Ordered on 6 July 1944, it was to be a patrol bomber powered by two P&W R-4360 radials and two 3825 lb thrust Allison J33-A-17 turbojets, paired in nacelles. Only 19 were produced, deliveries starting on 28 June 1950 to VP-21. The Mercator had a top speed of 410 mph at 21,000 ft, span of 114 ft, length of 84 ft and gross weight of 83,378 lb. However, the spacious fuselage and high top speed led the Navy to convert most of the production run to P4M-1Q configuration for ELINT squadrons VQ-1 and VQ-2. BuNo 124364 was assigned to VQ-1 and photographed on 2 July 1960 at Alameda NAS.

104. Equipped with a wide variety of intelligence gathering gear, the P4M-Qs flew sorties from bases in Japan in and around the Chinese and Russian borders, sensitive equipment recording many details of considerable use to Allied intelligence. The top turret with the .50 caliber machine guns was deleted but the 20mm nose and tail turrets were invaluable against border defenses.

103

104

105. The North American AJ-1 Savage gave the US Navy its first strategic nuclear bomber, the first XAJ-1 flying on 3 July 1948, powered by two 2300 hp P&W R-2800-44W radials. The unarmed bomber entered service with VC-5 in September 1949, but had limited use since rapidly developing jet fighters made its reliance on speed defense uncertain. The next version was the AJ-2P photo recon aircraft (30 built). The bomb bay area could house up to seven cameras and the aircraft was equipped for day and night photography, the ports clearly visible in this banking view. A bulbous nose also housed cameras.

106. One of the Navy's most useful and longest-lived recon platforms is the Douglas Skywarrior. First flying on 28 October 1952, the A3D-1 was designed as the Navy's first jet-powered nuclear bomber, but gained true fame in the sky spy mission. The prototype YA3D-2P first flew on 22 July 1958 and was followed by 29 production variants (BuNo 142666 illustrated). The A3D-2P (later RA-3B) had the bomb bay area replaced by a pressurized compartment for two cameramen and up to 12 cameras.

107. The Douglas Skyraider came about as Douglas designed an aircraft to meet a new category of Naval warplane: the BT class, a single-seater combining dive and torpedo bombing. The resulting XBT2D-1 was a very large single engine machine powered by a Wright R-3350-24W of 2500 hp. It first flew on 18 March 1945. Right from the start, the Navy and Douglas knew they had a winner. The Navy had ordered

25; these were accepted by the Navy during June 1945 to May 1948. Many were modified for other roles. BuNo 09096 was converted by Douglas as the XBT2D-1P, a prototype for a single-seat photo recon machine. Fairings on the rear fuselage held camera positions and the necessary ports while other cameras were added to shoot vertically. The XBT2D-1P is illustrated at the Long Beach factory as cameras are installed for a test.

108. The BT designation was replaced after the prototypes by the new AD attack designation. The AD-4W (illustrated) was a three-seat AEW aircraft; 168 were constructed, mainly for the USN but 50 went to the Royal Navy. Two crew members inside the fuselage operated the AN/APS-20 search radar in the large pod under the fuselage. The first 52 were also configured for ASW but this requirement was later dropped.

107

109. Another variant of the prolific Skyraider series was the electronic warfare (EWf) AD-5Q (redesignated EA-1F in 1962). Powered by a Wright R-3350-26WA, the AD-5Q had a crew of four, three systems operators and one pilot. Featuring a longer fuselage (40 ft 1 in) and a greatly expanded cockpit area, it came about as a modification kit supplied by the factory and for the AD-5N airframe; 53 were converted. Capable of carrying a wide variety of electronic countermeasures (ECM) equipment, the AD-5Q saw service with such squadrons as VAW-11, VAW-33, VAW-35, and VAQ-33. The pod under the right wing of the illustrated AD-5Q is an electronic countermeasures unit. This AD-5Q belonged to a detachment of VAW-33 and was based at NAS Quonset Point where it was photographed on 6 September 1962.

110 The AD-5W (redesignated EA-1E in 1962) was the AEW variant of the AD-5 series, equipped with a very large belly radome to house the AN/APS-20 search radar manned by two operators. It was not a small machine, but capable of a top speed of 299 mph. The AD-5W (218 built) served with VAW-11, VAW-12, VAW-33 (illustrated) and VMCJ-3. As the final AEW variant, the AD-5W served in the Vietnam War.

109

110

6

LANDFORD WAR
PHOTO-FILES

THE LOCKHEED
U-2 AND SR-71
BLACKBIRD

111. The aircraft that started the modern American revolution in aerial espionage, the prototype Lockheed U-2 (code-named Article 341) parked at the joint USAF/CIA flight test center at Groom Lake, Nevada, probably during late July 1955 before the first flight. The vast expanse and remoteness of Groom Lake made it an ideal testing site for clandestine projects—a role in which it continues today.

112. Article 341 differed in a number of ways from the production run of the U-2s. Virtually handbuilt by select Lockheed 'Skunk Works' personnel, it made its first official flight from Groom Lake on 1 August 1955 (a couple of unintentional 'hops' had occurred during taxi trials) flown by veteran test pilot Tony LeVier. The prototype was a handful, more like a European high-performance glider than a military jet.

National insignia were added to mask the identity of the true purchaser: the Central Intelligence Agency. Some sources speculate that the 001 coding on the fin was airbrushed on the negative, but, examination of an original print under extremely heavy magnification indicates that it was painted on the fin.

111

114

112

113

113. Article 341 in yet another guise: NACA 320. An examination of this photograph (not an original print) suggests that the CIA painted the aircraft with this fictitious and benign identity in case the photograph ever had to be used, immediately stripping off the paint after the negative was exposed. The prototype had a turbojet P&W J57 optimized for high altitude operations: an uncharted area.

114 With speed brakes popped to slow down for formation with the photo plane, a Central Intelligence Agency U-2B displays the red 'wing walk' stripes atop the huge wing. However, the wing was so fragile that ground crewmen could not walk on them as with other military aircraft, and the stripes served basically to outline wing structure. The U-2B was photographed after modifications at Lockheed's Van Nuys plant,

California, during the mid-1960s. Once again it carries the spurious civil registration N809X which was used during operations out of Van Nuys—the world's busiest civil airport. The rather incredible concept of having ultra-secret aircraft operate out of such a busy civilian airport gives a curious insight into the bureaucratic mind. N809X shows the various modifications introduced at Van Nuys.

115. Designer Kelly Johnson, posing by the wing-tip of a CIA U-2A carrying the absolutely meaningless American civil registration N803X. The fact that the CIA was the original customer and funder for the Lockheed U-2 project did not prevent the USAF from taking an immediate and active interest in the aircraft and its capabilities. The main objective of the CIA U-2 program was to keep Soviet military / missile operations under as close surveillance as possible. President Dwight D. Eisenhower was perplexed about the clandestine nature of the aircraft's operation but finally gave permission for the overflights since he considered them to be in the nation's best interest.

116. The most famous U-2 pilot of all time, Francis Gary Powers had the misfortune of being shot down by a Russian SAM-2 during a spy flight by U-2B 56-6693 over Sverdlovsk from the CIA base in Pakistan on 1 May 1960 (the Communist May Day could not have been a worse day for international publicity regarding the downing of an American spy). Almost overnight, the U-2 was withdrawn into the shadows.

115

117

116

118

117. U-2 56-6700 was built as an A model and then converted to C model standards. It is seen in a very distinctive two-tone grey camouflage scheme (known as 'Broken Sky'). According to some sources, this scheme was specially requested by the British government to help dispel some of the U-2's 'sinister' reputation when deployed to Britain in the mid-1970s to test a new system for locating Soviet radars.

118 A classic study of U-2A 56-6708 during the late 1950s with USAF unit citation insignia on the vertical fin. Assigned to the 4080th SRW, 56-6708 participated in the historic Cuban overflights during 1962. President John Kennedy, amid growing concern that the Soviets might be heavily fortifying Cuba, authorized a weekly U-2 overflight of the island. It was during a three-week moratorium that the first ship loaded with Russian medium range ballistic missiles arrived in Cuba. The overflights began once again during the first week of October 1962 with CIA pilots. On 10 October, USAF pilots took over the mission and on 14 October Major Steve Heyser's overflight recorded the images of the Soviet missiles and sites for radar and launchers.

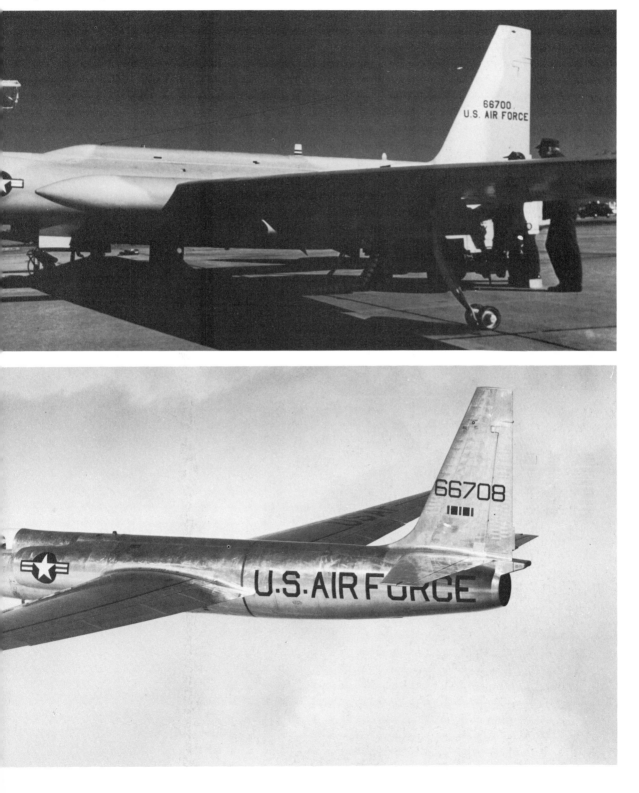

119. Bare metal U-2A 56-6703 displays the early-style USAF markings applied to the aircraft. The intakes on the U-2A were fairly simple affairs, but they became much more bulged with the U-2C modification. At first thought virtually invulnerable to early Soviet surface-to-air missiles, after the Powers incident various missile warning devices were added. A sheet metal structure added to the bottom portion of the exhaust pipe helped diffuse the infrared signature coming from the hot exhaust, thus confusing heat-seeking missiles.

120. Formation view of U-2D 56-6722 (foreground) and U-2A 56-6701 over Edwards AFB, California, when they were assigned to the 6512th Test Group, USAF Air Research and Development Command (ARDC). 6722 was assigned to PROJECT SMOKEY JOE—the program to develop effective American spy satellites and to come up with an effective Missile Defense Alarm System (MIDAS). Testing took place in the early 1960s, with MIDAS sensors mounted atop the fuselage, the sensor theoretically being able to detect the size and type of an enemy missile launch against the United States. After several unsuccessful years the program was terminated.

119

120

121. Speed brakes deployed, 6722 entering the downwind for landing at a USAF base. The red and white HICAT probe (nicknamed 'barber's pole') identifies its mission. Much of the high altitude turbulence data gathered by 6722 was of use in the Concorde supersonic transport program. The configuration of 6722 has changed once again, the hump over the second seat position giving way to the smaller fairing.

122. The final paint scheme applied to 56-6722 was this elegant overall white finish with red trim. In the 1970s, it was used by the Air Force Flight Test Center (AFFTC) for familiarization and other less strenuous roles. It was modified to look almost like a U-2C with single-seat configuration and the long dorsal spine common to the C model. 6722 now has a place of honour at the United States Air Force Museum, Dayton.

121

123. The CIA used NACA (to become NASA in 1958) as a convenient cover for their clandestine U-2 operations. However, NASA eventually did get to utilize U-2s for their own purposes when, on 2 April 1971, two U-2Cs were transferred from the USAF to NASA at Ames Research Center, Moffett NAS. They were given civil registrations N708NA (56-6681) and N709NA (56-6682) and a new name, Earth Resources Survey Aircraft.

124. U-2D 56-6954 seen shortly after touchdown, with wings still level. The aircraft displays the curious 'black and silver' paint scheme common to some of the U-2s. Assigned to the 6512th Test Group at Edwards when the photograph was taken in 1964, some sources state that this aircraft was converted to U-2C configuration before being assigned to the 100th SRW, eventually disappearing from USAF records.

125. U-2A 56-6721 had a long and useful USAF career, eventually being modified to U-2D configuration with a second seat and various optical sensors. The U-2A had a length of 49 ft 8.6 in and a wing span of 80 ft 2 in. This view of 6721 shows the aircraft positioned for take-off, its outriggers keeping the wing level. A large sensor is mounted between the seats.

123

124

125

126. U-2s based at Edwards have also been used for a wide variety of photographic calibration testing. High resolution cameras were installed on special mountings at Edwards to track the U-2 as it passed over at various altitudes.

127. Heavy attrition with the U-2 force and dropping the USAF's COMPASS COPE remotely piloted vehicle program led the service into discussing with Lockheed-California producing a new, much improved version of the U-2. The resulting aircraft, the U-2R, was about 40 percent larger overall and had a stronger airframe, better controls and increased payload, but retained the J75. It first flew on 28 August 1967.

128. U-2R 68-10329 equipped with large wing 'super pods' more common to the TR-1 series of aircraft. With the U-2R series, the CIA and the USAF went to absolutely minimum markings. A great deal of confusion (not uncommon among any of the U-2 series) surrounds the exact number of U-2Rs built.

126

127

128

129. Undersurface view of U-2R 68-10339 before assignment to the 100th SRW during early 1969, showing the long wing span of the R (103 ft). The fuselage length, normally 62 ft 9 in, can vary depending on the type of nose carried for a specific mission. Loaded mission weight is around 41,000 lb—almost double the U-2A's 22,000 lb. Some operated out of Taiwan have been seen with small Nationalist Chinese insignia.

130. U-2R 68-10339, after service with the CIA, 100th SRW and 9th SRW, went on to be assigned to the US Navy for the U-2 EP-X (Electronics Patrol-Experimental) program. Two U-2Rs were modified during 1973 to carry the electronics equipment that the Navy desired—gear that would closely monitor surface shipping from a high altitude. Two large pods were built by Lockheed for FLIR while other associated

equipment was carried in the storage bays. The paint scheme was standard matte black with large white Navy on the fuselage sides. After Navy service, 10339 went to the Air Force where it was modified with a variety of ELINT sensors and SLAR.

129

131. One of the more interesting uses for the U-2R was during 1969 when Lockheed pilot Bill Park carrier qualified the R aboard USS *America*, CVA-66. From 21 through 23 November, in secret tests off the Virginia coast, he demonstrated there was no doubt the U-2R could be recovered by a carrier, bringing it aboard at 72 knots while *America* steamed at 20 knots.

132. *America* deck crewmen disengage the U-2R's hook from the cable while Park remains in the cockpit for another try. The CIA had carried out carrier operations with U-2As in the early 1960s so the concept was not entirely new. Although the U-2R's carrier testing has been declassified, the exact nature of the mission has not. The R did not need the standard catapult launch.

133. One of the strangest U-2Rs flying, 68-10336, modified with a greatly extended nose radome, served as a flying test bed for a large SLAR, which would be extremely useful if the U-2R was patrolling near the border of Warsaw Pact countries, allowing for extremely deep penetration and observation of WarPac activities without entailing overflight.

132

131

133

134. With increasing demands on its limited numbers of U-2s, the USAF and Lockheed entered discussions about reopening the production line. In 1978, details of the program were made public along with the new aircraft's designation: TR-1A. Basically a new U-2R with minor differences (it was felt that the TR designation—Tactical Recon—was more politically acceptable than U-2), the TR-1A would accommodate Hughes Advanced Synthetic Aperture Radar System (ASARS) along with a new SLAR. Precision Emitter Location Strike System (PLSS) had been developed by Lockheed to allow TR-1As to gather information about hostile forces while orbiting over friendly territory. The information would be instantly transmitted to a ground station so that the new data would be available to battlefield commanders.

135. TR-1A number 2, 80-1067, on a test flight near Palmdale. The USAF may procure up to 25 although budget cut backs may reduce or at least spread out deliveries. With this number of TR-1As and older and replacement U-2Rs, the USAF feels that its world-wide strategic recon mission can be met. Work on the actual prototype TR-1A began in late 1979 and the rollout of the first aircraft, during July 1981.

136. Without its wing-mounted super pods, this TR-1A looks just like the U-2R from whence it came. Though the U-2R/TR-1A series has a stronger airframe than the original U-2, its glider-like structure is still rather delicate and prone to damage. Many severely damaged U-2s have come back to 'life' via extensive rebuilding since the structure is relatively simple and lends itself to remanufacture.

137. TR-1A 80-1067 heads directly at the camera plane, gust flaps slightly deployed. The huge wing is very resilient and can 'flap' up and down several feet in turbulence. With its super pods, extended nose and equipment bays, the TR-1A can carry over 4,000 lb of state-of-the-art intelligence equipment. 80-1067 operates with the 9th SRW out of Beale AFB.

135

136

137

138. Banking steeply near Malibu, California, the pilot of the first TR-1B passes under the photo plane. Earlier U-2CT dual control trainers have now been withdrawn from service, leaving the training task to the specially-built TR-1Bs. The all-white finish is typical of aircraft operating in the USAF training mission.

139. In order to facilitate TR-1A crew training, the initial contract specified two dual control training versions to be built. Designated TR-1B, they were to be assigned to the 9th SRW at Beale AFB. Assigned to the 4080th SRTS (Strategic Reconnaissance Training Squadron) within the 9th, the aircraft retains a limited operational role. 80-1064 was the first TR-1B built.

140. The original contract for the TR-1A specified a 42.4 million dollar price for the construction of two TR-1As for the USAF and one ER-2 (with sensitive military items eliminated) for NASA, augmenting the two U-2Cs operated by them. The first ER-2 (80-1063, N706NA) rolled out from Palmdale for its first flight on 11 May 1981, and was delivered to NASA on 10 June.

139

140

141. The horizontal stabilizer of a TR-1A in the construction jig. As with the rest of the TR-1A airframe, the structure is light and simple and somewhat akin to non-composite glider construction. Elevator travel is 20 degrees down, 30 degrees up. Views of Lockheed spy aircraft under construction are not common. However, in recent years the company has released a few photos of U-2R/TR-1 construction at Burbank.

142. Lockheed worker examines a TR-1A equipment bay; the engine intake is clearly visible. The U-2/TR-1A series embodied Kelly Johnson's dictum of 'keep it simple': construction is very basic, making repairs much less complicated than other USAF aircraft—one of the reasons that early U-2s gave such long service. Since the aircraft are ordered in such limited numbers, each is virtually handmade.

143. Tail wheel assembly for the TR-1A shows the unit's extremely rugged construction along with the solid rubber tires. The TR-1 is the only aircraft (along with the U-2R) in the USAF inventory to utilize the tandem landing gear arrangement.

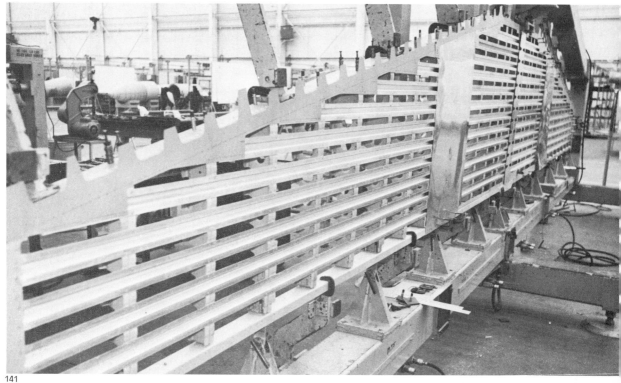

141

142

144. The forward fuselage section of the first TR-1A being moved out of its jig for final assembly. This was the first U-2 type aircraft to be made completely new in almost twelve years. The fuselage section is finished in zinc chromate primer.

145. The forward fuselage of the first TR-1B is seen in its jig (note the raised accommodation for the second seat). Lockheed's tooling is such that the TR-1/U-2R can be brought in and out of production with relative ease since the tooling is kept in storage and the method of construction is rapid.

143

144

145

146. The Lockheed series of high-performance strategic reconnaissance aircraft has remained the most classified aircraft program in American aeronautical history, although the new 'stealth' aircraft currently being built will rival the 'Blackbirds'. The first machine in the Lockheed series was the A-12, a single-seat aircraft optimized for high speed and long range, built with massive funding from the CIA. The first A-12 flight took place at the secret Groom Lake, Nevada, test facility on 26 April 1962. Three dedicated interceptors (YF-12As) were developed from the A-12 project. The A-12 was reported to have a top speed of 2400 mph at around 95,000 ft and was capable of carrying more advanced and heavier equipment than the earlier U-2. It is thought a dozen A-12s were constructed. The type was withdrawn from service in 1968. Around eight are in long-term storage at Palmdale, California. This is the only official, and heavily retouched, photograph released by Lockheed of the A-12.

146

147. The only—and heavily retouched—photographs released illustrating the unusual combination of Lockheed A-12 and D-21 drone. The aircraft is 60-6940, one of two modified to two seat configuration to accommodate the drone operator behind the pilot; one being destroyed during an attempted launch. Carrying recon equipment, the D-21, another CIA-funded program, would be launched into heavily defended areas for reconnaissance. The program was not a success when mated to the A-12 and carriage was switched to two modified Boeing B-52Hs of the 4200th Test Wing at Beale AFB, for clandestine missions.

148. Captain Robert C. Helt (pilot) and Major Larry A. Elliott (RSO), who set world altitude records in the SR on 27 July 1976, in front of an SR-71A. Crews wear S1010B full-pressure suits. The SR set the height record at 85,069 ft, and has set numerous speed records, many of which still stand.

149. William C. Park, long associated with Lockheed's 'black projects', is seen standing next to an SR-71A after being awarded the Octave Chanute Award for 'flight test development of Mach 3-plus aircraft' during March 1969. Park, who holds the distinction of being the first test pilot to fly the SR-71 and YF-12A aircraft at their design speed, is shown in the pressure suit worn by Blackbird crews. The SR-71A was a logical follow-on to the A-12. The systems carried by the A-12 were so complex that the pilot's work load was almost impossible and the SR-71A's second seat made room for a Reconnaissance Systems Officer (RSO). The SR, a major redesign of the earlier aircraft, was developed in security equal to the A-12. The contract for the first six SRs was issued in December 1962. The first flight of the prototype took place on 22 December 1964.

150. A high-angle view of SR-71A 64-17976 in flight in July 1979. This aircraft is assigned to the 1st Strategic Reconnaissance Squadron, Beale Air Force Base, California.

151. An SR-71A with its two P&W J58 32,500 lb thrust engines at full thrust in afterburner squeezes the moisture out the atmosphere as it takes off on a mission.

152. The dual control SR-71B trainer became the first SR to complete 1000 missions and was suitably marked for its historic flight during February 1982. Three training variants of the SR have been built, two Bs and one C, but 64-17956 is the only one still operational. The elevated rear cockpit is clearly visible.

150

151

152

153. Nose held high, SR-71A 64-17956 touches down at Palmdale, California. Assigned to Lockheed for advanced modification work, '956 carries the famous 'Skunk Works' insignia on the tail. Pilots keep the nose high during the landing run to increase aerodynamic drag in order to slow the fast-landing aircraft down. Blackbirds are powered by two P&W J58 of 32,500 lb thrust each. The designation should have been 'RS-71'

but President Johnson, in another of his public speech mistakes, referred to the machine as the 'SR-71' on 24 July 1964 and, oddly, the designation stuck.

154. SR-71A 64-17955 refuelling from a Boeing KC-135Q shortly after take-off. Beale has a strictly SR-dedicated tanker unit assigned. SRs use JP-7 fuel (over 12,000 US gallons carried internally), optimized for the high altitudes and high speeds at which it operates. All SRs now carry very low visibility markings in contrast to this aircraft's white markings.

153

154

7

BLANDFORD WAR
PHOTO-FILES

THE
VIETNAM ERA-
US NAVY

155. The camera-equipped F8U-1P entered Navy and Marine Corps service as a replacement for the F9F-8P Cougar, its gun bays and forward fuselage modified to house a battery of five cameras shooting through optically corrected armor glass ports in the sides and belly, two mounted vertically and three in trimetrogon mounts capable of producing horizon-to-horizon panoramic strip photographs.

156. One of the most powerful jet fighters to see service with the US Navy, the Chance Vought Crusader gave the Navy supersonic capabilities and an aircraft that was able to become an effective MiG killer over Vietnam during that lengthy conflict. The Crusader, however, was modified into another very important role: photo reconnaissance, and this variant outlived the air superiority day fighter in Navy service.

Camera-equipped F8U-1Ps entered service with the Navy's light photographic reconnaissance squadrons during 1957 with VFP-61 at NAS Miramar, California, and VFP-62 at NAS Cecil Field, Florida. This climbing view of a VFP-61 Crusader shows off the modified forward fuselage, area-ruled to counteract drag generated by the squared-off camera bay.

155

156

157. Based at NAS Cecil Field, Florida, VFP-62 was responsible for carrying out photographic reconnaissance missions for ships attached to the Sixth Fleet and deploying in the Mediterranean. It was one of two squadrons—the other being VMCJ-2—which operated from NAS Jacksonville, Florida, on low-level missions over Cuba during the Missile Crisis of October 1962.

158. On 18 September 1966, an RF-8 penetrated North Vietnamese airspace at supersonic speed to photograph the partial effect of about 200 tons of bombs dropped by Air Wing 15 Intruders and Skyhawks on a large railroad complex northeast of Thanh Hoa. At least eight AA sites were knocked out.

159. Photo Crusaders were so useful to the Fleet that, in 1965, Vought began a remanufacturing program to extend their service life, 73 being processed. These RF-8Gs were rugged, capable machines that could penetrate the well-defended areas of North Vietnam to bring back valuable information. Changes included strengthened wings, with drooping outboard leading edges and A-7-based landing gear.

157

158

159

One of the most interesting combat Naval aircraft to be developed during the 1950s was the North American Aviation A-5 Vigilante. One of the heaviest aircraft ever to be accepted for duty aboard an aircraft carrier, the Vigilante, originally designated A3J, was designed as a high-performance, all-weather attack machine. Loaded with advanced aerodynamic features, the aircraft flew for the first time on 31 August 1958, with deliveries to the first operational unit, VAH-7, starting in 1961. A linear bomb bay was located between the tail pipes of the J79 engines and a free-falling nuclear weapon could be ejected towards the rear. This system, along with the fact that two empty fuel tanks would be ejected with the weapon to stabilize its fall, gave the Navy plenty of developmental headaches. Around this time, the Navy revised its mission to exclude strategic bombing and an advanced A-5B was put on hold but, in a search for an advanced recon aircraft, the A-5B's features were incorporated into the new RA-5C. Capable of carrying a large amount of electronic and photographic gear in the bomb bay, the RA-5C also had SLAR in a large fairing on the fuselage, split image, vertical and oblique cameras, along with active and passive ECM equipment.

160. An RA-5C takes on fuel from an A-3B Skywarrior while overflying the USS *Ranger* (CVA-61) on 6 August 1964. Unrefuelled, the RA-5C had a combat radius of 547 miles on internal fuel or 944 miles when carrying four 400 US gallon under wing fuel tanks. As North Vietnam's AA defences improved, even the RA-5C's high top speed could not prevent losses to advanced Russian SAMs. The addition of chaff and flare units along with new ECM equipment helped to counter the threat in the increasingly hostile skies. The first RA-5C flew on 30 June 1962.

161. An RA-5C of RVAH-3 (Reconnaissance Heavy Attack) displays the huge SLAR unit under the fuselage.

162. The RA-5C proved to be such a valuable reconnaissance tool for the Navy that, during 1964, work began to convert 43 A-5As (59 had been built) to RA-5C standard; 91 new RA-5Cs were built. The first squadron to receive the type was RVAH-5; other units to receive the type included RVAH-1, 7, 9 and 11. The RA-5C was powered by two 10,800 lb static thrust General Electric J79-GE-8 turbojets that gave the aircraft a maximum speed of 1380 mph (Mach 2.1) at 40,000 ft. An RA-5C is seen recovering aboard the USS *Constellation* (CVA-64) on 15 May 1969.

161

163. With the nose wheel steering hard left, the pilot of this RVAH-6 RA-5C Vigilante gently advances the throttles as he moves the 55,600 lb aircraft toward the deck crewman guiding the aircraft towards a catapult aboard the USS *Forrestal*. The side looking radar (SLAR) under the fuselage could be employed when flying parallel to an unfriendly nation's border, enabling the RA-5C to 'look' deep inside hostile territory while flying over safe airspace. With its high landing speed, the RA-5C was a tricky aircraft to land on carriers.

164. A Photographer's Mate loading film into the forward camera station on an RA-5C assigned to RVAH-6 aboard the attack carrier USS *Forrestal* (CVA-57) during 1974. When the Vigilante was flying at its combat ceiling of 48,000 ft, the advanced cameras aboard the RA-5C could record huge chunks of territory.

163

164

165. Flight of RVAH-7 RA-5Cs. The large fuselage hump carried additional fuel while more fuel or ECM pods (illustrated) could be carried underwing. The only Mach 2 recon aircraft ever operated from a carrier, the RA-5C was widely deployed in Vietnam, and at least 18 were lost in combat. The last was delivered on 5 November 1970, the type being phased out of service completely by 1981.

166. The Douglas F3D Skyknight was built as an all-weather fighter for the Navy and Marines. Its brief career was highlighted by scoring the first jet versus jet night kill, during the Korean War. During the early 1960s, 35 F-10B (F3D-2 was redesignated in 1962) airframes were converted to EF-10B EWf/ELINT aircraft, which immediately performed valuable work ferreting out radar installations the Russians had built in Cuba during

1962—the beginning of the Cuban Missile Crisis. In April 1965, VMCJ-1 was deployed to Da Nang, South Vietnam. Their EWf/ELINT operations over four years resulted in the destruction of enemy radars and stockpiles. The type was phased out during the 1970s. The VMCJ-1 EF-10B illustrated has over 400 EWf/ELINT missions recorded by lightning bolts.

165

166

167. Known as Warning Stars, the US Navy's WV-2s were fitted with 600 US gallon tip tanks for extra range. Early variants carried a crew of 32 but gradual modernization of equipment reduced crew size to 28. WV-2s were redesignated EC-121K with the September 1962 Tri-Service designation scheme (see **190**).

168. Very well-worn Warning Star in overall faded Glossy Sea Blue, photographed on 8 December 1962 at New York International Airport, still carrying its old WV-2 designation rather than the newer EC-121K. BuNo 143184 was assigned to the Glynco Naval Air Reserve. Reserve Warning Stars operated in conjunction with fleet squadrons, conducting training and intercept exercises.

169. One of the strangest Warning Star modifications was the JC-121K-LO, a conversion of EC-121K BuNo 143196. Assigned to the US Army, it was used for many years to test a variety of classified sensor and detecting equipment. Many observation and sighting ports were built into the fuselage. The huge hump could house larger testing equipment. It was overall white with orange trim.

167

168

169

170. One of the US Navy's most famous ASW aircraft was the rugged and dependable Grumman S2F (redesignated S-2 during 1962) tracker series, a successful attempt to replace the unwieldy hunter/killer two-plane ASW system. The first XS2F flew on 4 December 1952. Powered by two Wright R-1820-82 Cyclones, it was equipped with radar-detecting ALD-3, APS-38 radar in a retractable radome for detecting surface objects and ASQ-10 MAD (Magnetic Anomaly Detection) gear in the tail with a long retractable sensor. Sonobuoys were carried in the rear of the engine nacelles, rockets and missiles under the wing and a torpedo in the bomb bay. The pilots were located in the extreme nose under large bulged windows which offered excellent visibility. A crew of two to four was carried in the fuselage. Many variants were produced for the US Navy and foreign governments. This classic photograph shows an S-2D with its MAD equipment extended as the crew searches a vast section of ocean for elusive submarines during an August 1961 exercise.

171. Sonobuoys being loaded in the rear nacelle of an S-2E, BuNo 152365. These were ejected over an area of ocean in which an enemy submarine

was suspected of operating. They picked up noises associated with submarine operations, relaying them to the Tracker for interpretation. Trackers could initiate an attack either using their weapons or by calling upon other Fleet elements. No longer in American service (except the C-1 Trader COD variant), Trackers still operate with several other nations, including Argentina who briefly used theirs in the South Atlantic War.

172. So great was the utility of the basic Tracker Trader airframe that Grumman developed the WF-2 (redesignated E-1B in 1962) as an AEW platform. Retaining the basic Trader configuration, a huge radome for the AN/APS-82 search radar—the 17 ft 6 in antenna inside rotated at six revolutions per minute—and a new 'triple' tail to overcome aerodynamic effects of the radome were added. The E-1B carried two

radar operators in the fuselage. First flown on 1 March 1957, the E-1B became operational during 1960, eventually being replaced by the much more advanced E-2 Hawkeye. By the mid-1970s, all had been withdrawn from service and scrapped at Davis-Monthan AFB, Arizona. Beside the prototype, 88 production E-1Bs were built.

171

The Grumman A-6 Intruder has proven to be one of the Navy's hardest hitting attack aircraft. With its all-weather capability, the A-6 series saw plenty of action during the Vietnam War, when its heavy weapons carrying ability was particularly appreciated. Grumman and the Navy developed a cost-effective EWf/ELINT A-6 airframe, designated EA-6B. The first aircraft (BuNo 149481) was flown on 25 May 1968, immediately identifiable by the extended forward fuselage housing the pilot and three systems operators. Using some of the systems from the earlier EA-6A (with a standard two-seat cockpit), the B model carried many more advanced systems including ALQ-99 EWf system, AN/ALQ-99 jamming system with five external transmitting pods, AN/ALQ-41 radar track-breaker and AN/ALQ-92 communications jammer. The initial EA-6B aircraft (three development prototypes, five production prototypes and 23 production machines) were designated BASIC to quantify their mission and capabilities (ability to operate in three bands against specific threats), but were updated to serve with more advanced EA-6Bs. Costing over $40 million each, the EA-6B is a limited production aircraft.

173. Fleet airpower at its best: an EA-6B Prowler surrounded by A-6E Intruders, an E-2C Hawkeye, A-7 Corsair IIs and F-4J Phantoms aboard USS *Nimitz* during NATO training exercises in September 1975, showing the Navy's mixed force of interceptor, EW, EWf/ELINT and attack aircraft. The EA-6B is not a small aircraft. Powered by two J52-P-408 turbojets, with a top speed of 613 mph, it has a take-off weight of 54,400 lb.

174. An EA-6B assigned to VAQ-132 in formation with an attack A-6E Intruder, BuNo 154159, from VA-165. (Grumman/777606-1)

175. This take-off view of an EA-6B shows the greatly expanded forward fuselage. The Prowler has had many updates (including addition of new-built machines) since it entered service, and around 80 are currently operational with the Fleet. It has a poor safety record (probably due to operating in any sort of weather); for instance, between November 1979 and February 1980, ten were lost, 18 crewmen being killed. The Prowler flew well over 700 combat missions in the closing stages of the Vietnam War, its advanced EWf/ELINT capabilities undoubtedly useful during the massive LINEBACKER II USAF B-52 bombing raids.

174

The Lockheed OP-2E Neptune, another specialized aircraft developed for service in the Vietnam War, was designed to deliver highly specialized units such as ADSIS, Acoubuoy, Spikebuoy and other sensors at advantageous positions along enemy trails so that vibrations from enemy movements could be picked up and studied for possible military reaction as part of IGLOO WHITE mission. Two test airframes and 12 operational OP-2Es were obtained during 1966-67 and assigned to VO-67 operating out of Nakhom Phanom, Thailand. Originally highly classified, the OP-2E crews were required to fly at low altitude in order to place their sensors accurately, making the lumbering Neptune an excellent target for the enemy's very effective AA fire. Three Neptunes were quickly lost in these operations and the Navy had to reconsider the type's combat role, eventually withdrawing the Neptune in favour of helicopters and jets. The airframe was heavily modified for the role, the large tail boom being lobbed off, and two SUU-11A/1A Minigun pods were installed underwing and ALE-29 chaff/flare dispensers in the rear fuselage to provide some AA suppression.

176. An overall green OP-2E of VO-67 in flight low over Thailand in December 1967.

177. A carefully camouflaged Spikebuoy sensor is loaded into a canister on an OP-2E for delivery to the Ho Chi Minh Trail. The large national insignia has been toned down so that the VC would not have a large aiming point. APQ-131 radar was installed in a chin radome.

178. The Orion can carry mines, torpedoes, nuclear and conventional depth bombs and rockets in the forward bomb bay or on wing pylons and sonobuoys and markers in the aft fuselage. P-3As carry Martin Bullpups underwing and later variants Harpoons.

179. The much more advanced Lockheed P-3 Orion (redesignated from P3V in 1962) replaced the Neptune. First entering service with VP-8 during 1962, it has remained one of the most potent ASW aircraft through constant equipment updates. In 1957, Lockheed proposed a modified Electra airliner to the Navy for the ASW role. Well over 500 have been built, including 157 P-3As with four 4500 hp Allison T56-A-10W turboprops. The main ASW gear included APS-80 radar, ASQ-10 MAD and an ASR-3.

178

179

180. VP-17 P-3B passing near the Soviet 'Chilikin' class fleet replenishment ship *Vladimir Kolechitsky* on 11 September 1974 during a routine Pacific patrol. With 4910 hp Allison T56-A-14 engines and advanced Deltic detection gear, Lockheed built 124 P-3Bs for the USN and others for the RAAF, RNZAF and Norway.

181. The very advanced P-3C entered service in 1969, first assigned to VP-30. Currently the Fleet's main fixed base ASW aircraft, earlier models being assigned to the Naval Air Reserve, the P-3C's main equipment includes an APS-115B search radar, ASQ-81 MAD gear, AQA-7 Directional Acoustics-Frequency Analysis and Recording unit (DIFAR) and AQH-4 multi-track sonar tape recorder. It has undergone three updates.

182. US Navy weather reconnaissance squadrons have always been associated with the intelligence gathering role. This WP-3A Orion BuNo 149674, seen on 10 June 1971, was assigned to VW-4. The WP-3A replaced Lockheed WC-121N and four stock P-3A airframes (BuNos 149674 / 149676) were modified for the mission, deleting MAD equipment. They were later converted to NP-3A and VP-3A configuration.

180

181

182

8

LANDFORD WAR
PHOTO-FILES

THE
VIETNAM ERA-
US AIR FORCE

The agile English Electric Canberra light bomber was built under license by Martin with many changes to conform to USAF operating techniques as the B-57A. The USAF early on planned a photo recon variant. By the end of 1954, RB-57As equipped the 363rd Tactical Reconnaissance Wing. From that point on, the versatile B-57 became one of the USAF's main modern spy planes. With the B-57 series, USAF intelligence gathering became an exact, and often deadly, science with spy planes venturing into the upper limits of the atmosphere over very hostile territory.

With the arrival of the RB-57D, the USAF sky spy role (under the direction of the Strategic Air Command) really started to change. The USAF wanted to modify an available aircraft to high altitude recon configuration and the example that would lend itself most readily to this modification was the B-57 since it had a spacious fuselage for equipment and offered good all-round performance. On 21 June 1954, the procurement of six B-57A aircraft began under the secret BLACK KNIGHT program. A massive new wing with a 106 ft span was designed and built to replace the 64 ft wing.

183

184

183. The first RB-57D-1 formates with a TAC night intruding B-57B; 20 Ds were built.

184. B-57B s/n 52-1498 at Sydney, Australia on 3 August 1965, while participating in an upper atmosphere survey. Equipped with wing tip sniffing pods, the B-57B would gather samples of air at high altitude for testing for radioactivity to detect atomic explosions.

185. This high angle view of an RB-57F shows the massive wing to advantage. Some were designated WB-57F for high altitude air sampling (HASP) missions and had a weather band painted across the vertical tail and a Military Air Transport Service (MATS) badge on to the vertical tail. Although MATS provisionally supervised these weather missions, many were actually CIA / USAF overflights of extremely sensitive areas.

186. Although the RB-57D was a radical modification, the basic design still had some stretch, amply illustrated with the RB-57F. Selected grounded RB-57Ds were transported to the General Dynamics facility in Fort Worth, Texas, totally taken apart and then rebuilt. Another new wing had been designed and built, spanning 122 ft, and two additional engines (J-60 turbojets) were slung underwing.

185

186

187. Nifty '50s all-weather airpower on parade. A USAF RC-121D leads a Northrop F-89D Scorpion, North American F-86D Sabre and Lockheed F-94 Starfire. Filled with electronic and radar equipment, the RC-121D's picket mission was to detect enemy aircraft long before they would be picked up by American coastal radar, and vector all-weather fighters. The USAF obtained 72 (redesignated EC-121Ds in 1962).

188. With the increasing sophistication of the Vietnam war, the USAF had 30 stored ex-Navy EC-121Ks and Ps modified to EC-121R-LOs by removing the radomes and AEW equipment and installing advanced sensors and relay equipment. Flown by the 553rd Reconnaissance Wing, Korat, Thailand, between October 1967 and December 1970, they analysed data from Beech QU-22Bs.

189. During the Vietnam War, the B-66 series really came into its own. In the mid-1960s 52 RB-66Bs were modified to EB-66E-DL status as active radar jammers. The tail turret was deleted and the bomb bay completely gutted, and replaced by the most advanced jamming equipment available. Chaff dispensing pods were mounted and the aircraft sprouted a veritable antenna farm.

187

188

189

190. Lockheed's Constellation series provided the basis for a long-lived fleet of spy planes. Ten RC-121C-LO AEW aircraft, constructed for the US Navy as the WV-2 were transferred to the USAF before acceptance by the Navy (51-3836/51-3845). Immediately indentifiable by the large radomes, they carried search radar to high altitudes to avoid radar's limitation of being unable to 'look over the horizon'. Not equipped with the most sophisticated equipment then available (to be carried by the RC-121D), they were redesignated TC-121C for AEW training. They had four 3400 hp Wright R-3350-34 radials.

191. The Douglas B-66 Destroyer provided the basis for several variants of reconnaissance and electronic warfare aircraft, its fuselage well-suited to the carriage of considerable amounts of equipment and cameras. The initial contract was for five RB-66As. The first flew on 28 June 1954 from Long Beach, California. The seven-seat RB-66C (illustrated) was an electronic reconnaissance and countermeasures platform. Four electronic warfare operators were located in the former bomb bay, now completely pressurized. The wingtip pods housed ECM. The first flew on 29 October 1955; 36 were built.

192. McDonnell F-101 Voodoo photographic variants gained their spurs during the Cuban Missile Crisis and the Vietnam War. Two YRF-101As were constructed during 1956. Production deliveries began in May 1957 to the 63rd Tactical Reconnaissance Wing. The RF-101C (illustrated) first flew on 12 July 1957 and was the last of the single-seat Voodoos (last delivery on 31 March 1959). The RF-101C (166 built) combined the F-101Cs stronger wing with the camera RF-101. A model photo nose carrying either four KA-2 for day operations or one KA-2 and three K-46 cameras for night use. Two KA-1s were mounted in a fuselage bay.

193. Much of the RF-101's mission in Vietnam was taken over by photo recon McDonnell Douglas Phantoms, the first of which was the RF-4B (originally F4H-1P), ordered into production in February 1963. Retaining the F-4Bs structure and two 10,900 lb thrust J79-GE-8 turbojets, it had a modified 4 ft 8 in longer nose with forward and side-oblique cameras or a mapping camera, and SLR and IR sensors. Photoflash bombs for night operations could be ejected from the fuselage. Film could be developed in flight and ejected to ground commanders. All 46 RF-4Bs built for the

192

Navy were assigned to the USMC. An RF-4B BuNo 153102 flown by Roy Stafford from VMFP-3 is illustrated.

194. The RF-4C is one of the most effective tactical reconnaissance aircraft in the USAF inventory. Two YRF-4C prototypes were flown in 1963 and 503 RF-4Cs were constructed. Powered by two J79-GE-15 engines, it has a top speed of 1459 mph, length of 62 ft 10⅞ in and a height of 16 ft 6 in. With advanced photo equipment in the nose, it is unarmed and either relies on its high top speed at low altitude or fighter and ECM protection for missions into heavily defended territory. This RF-4C-34-MC s/n 67-0448 was assigned to the 16th TRS/360th TRW at Tan Son Nhut Air Base in South Vietnam when it was photographed in 1970.

195. A technician removes film packs from the nose of an ANG RF-4C. The camera installation swings down and the forward portion of the nose hinges to the front for easy access to the camera bay. The RF-4C has three camera stations located in the nose, SLR, FLR and IR recon equipment. It can eject photoflash bombs and process and eject film in flight.

194

196. Republic F-105G Wild Weasel of the 35th Tactical Fighter Wing with practice munitions, including the short-range AGM-45 Shrike on the outboard pylon and the longer range AGM-78 Standard anti-radiation missile (ARM) on the inboard pylon. The F-105G had a built-in 20mm Gatling gun cannon. (USAF)

197. The hostile SAM environment over targets in North Vietnam brought about a requirement for an aircraft that could suppress SAM units. The two-seat Republic F-105F Thunderchief (whose single-seat variants were widely used during the war, suffering the heaviest loss ratio of any American warplane used during that conflict) was modified for the SAM suppression—or 'Wild Weasel'—mission. By the end of 1966, over

196

197

twenty Wild Weasels had been delivered to the USAF and work progressed on a more advanced version to be known as the EF-105F (later changed to F-105G), with the first operational aircraft arriving in Vietnam by the end of 1969. The F-105G was fitted with AN/ALQ-105 jamming equipment mounted on the fuselage. An Itek AN/ALR-46 system was able to detect up to sixteen emitters (impulses coming from SAM units) at one time while AN/APR-35 search/homing receiver would aid in locking onto the impulses coming from the launch site. The F-105G could carry a deadly load of weapons including AGM-45 and AGM-78 missiles capable of seeking out the SAM sites once the rear seater in the F-105G had located and locked on to the SAM site. The F-105 was completely retired from USAF inventory by 1984, being replaced by F-4Gs.

198. Lockheed EC-130Q Hercules operated out of NATC Patuxent River, Maryland, by Fleet Air Reconnaissance Squadron 4 (VQ-4), part of the TACAMO (Take Charge and Move Out) system. Their Hercules are modified C-103H airframes equipped with VLF (very low frequency) communications relay systems to guard against a major breakdown in military communications in the event of a national emergency or war. A long trailing antenna can be reeled out in flight; the receptacle can be seen in the rear ramp door. Note the modified wing tips common to the type.

199. Carrying the rather vague title 'Rescue', this HC-130H-LM was one of 43 built (s/n 64-14852/64-14866; 65-962/65-987; 65-989/65-990) by Lockheed-Georgia. A large streamlined radome on the forward fuselage housed re-entry tracking radar used to spot reconnaissance packages ejected from orbiting satellites. Proceeding to the area where the package was descending by parachute, they snagged the 'chute with the Fulton recovery system in the nose. This system was also used in recovering downed aircrew or clandestine agents. Two 1800 US gallon fuel tanks were carried underwing.

198

199

200. The Lockheed RC-130A Hercules was a conversion of the basic A model into a photo-mapping and recon platform. Initially, one TC-130A (54-1632) was converted, then a further 15 (57-510/57-524). The large cargo fuselage had more than enough room for cameras and mapping gear, extra ports being installed in the belly and side of the fuselage. Most were later reconverted to cargo configuration.

201. One of the more unusual modifications to which the versatile Hercules has been subjected: several different variants of the family have been modified to DC-130 configuration to carry long-range remotely piloted vehicles (RPVs) which have been built for either strike or reconnaissance missions. This DC-130E carries two very large high altitude RPVs which would be launched while the aircraft was still in friendly territory and then fly under guidance from the DC-130 to assigned targets in hostile territory, either relaying information back or to being recovered in friendly territory. During the Vietnam War, RPVs launched from DC-130s were extensively tested and used. Note the additional radome under the nose.

200

201

During 1950, Cessna Aircraft Corporation won a contract, with their Model 305A, to supply the Army with a new liaison aircraft. Designated L-19A, the little aircraft was based on the civil Model 170 and featured two tandem seats for a pilot and an observer in a cabin extensively surrounded by plexiglass. Large orders were placed so that the Army's liaison fleet could be updated and 2480 Bird Dogs, as the type had been named, were delivered by October 1954. Other contracts followed for more aircraft including the TL-19D trainer (310 built, and 376 L-19Es with an improved model of engine and updated equipment. Production finally ended in 1962. All-metal construction and spring steel landing gear made the Bird Dog a rugged and nimble performer. Seeing service during the Korean War, the L-19 (redesignated O-1 during the 1962 tri-service designation consolidation), the Bird Dog gained real fame during the Vietnam War where it became the main FAC aircraft. The FACs would spot possible Viet Cong targets and then call in fighter-bomber strikes with F-105s and F-4s. The Viet Cong came to detest the small aircraft and would usually open fire on a Bird Dog whenever the little aircraft were observed.

202. As the American involvement in the war grew, more advisors, aircraft and troops were shipped to Southeast Asia. This photograph shows FAC pilot Captain Lawrence L. Reed going over a mission with his Vietnamese observer. The two men were preparing to fly from their base at Song Ba Special Forces Camp in an O-1E painted overall grey to check on suspected Viet Cong positions near the camp.

203. Typical USAF FAC pilot ready for a mission with a Vietnamese Air Force (VNAF) O-1E, parked on a pierced steel planking (PSP) ramp. The VNAF's 2nd Liaison Squadron Star-and-Cobra insignia is seen painted on the door. The parachute, propped against the landing gear, was used as a seat cushion since the FACs operated at such low altitudes that the employment of a parachute was dubious.

204. With the upper portions of its wing banded in white to aid recognition for fighter-bombers, a VNAF O-1E cruises over one of the thousands of canals that criss-cross Vietnam and serve as highways for virtually all commercial traffic. Spanning 36 ft and 25 ft 9½ in long, with a 213 hp Continental O-470-11, the O-1E had a top speed of 151 mph at sea level.

203

205. An O-2A (s/n 68-11026) of the 21st TASS returns to Phu Cat Air Base, Vietnam, after an FAC mission in the local area. The O-2As were responsible for locating the many Russian-made 122mm rocket launchers that were bombarding the base. In need of a more combat suitable aircraft to replace the O-1, in the FAC mission in Southeast Asia, the USAF ordered 346 of a militarized variant of the Cessna 337 Skymaster,

designated O-2A. Unique in configuration, the 337 features twin 'push-pull' Continental 10-360-C/D piston engines. Though more powerful, (210 hp per engine) and faster (199 mph at sea level), than the O-1, it was still not the completely combat-worthy FAC aircraft that the USAF wanted. Prime targets for ground gunners, they were given four underwing pylons for light ordnance including 7.62mm Minigun packs.

206. O-2As were also flown on psychological warfare missions (PSYWAR) by the 9th Air Commando Squadron from Da Nang Air Base. The O-2A's first combat mission was the delivery of leaflets urging the Viet Cong to surrender. It rapidly became the primary psychological warfare aircraft for the I Corps area. O-2A spewing leaflets over an area held by the enemy, on 11 July 1967.

205

206

207. During the 1960s, Lockheed, the US government and the CIA set about to see if a 'silent' aircraft could be developed for clandestine duties. An aircraft that could fly relatively low over sensitive areas with virtual silence was felt to have considerable value in Vietnam. Accordingly, Lockheed obtained several airframes of Schweizer SGS-232 sailplanes and began extensively to modify them under the designation 'Q-Star'. A rotary combustion Wankel-type engine built by the Curtiss-Wright Corp. was mounted above and behind the cockpit while a ten-foot drive shaft drove a specially built multi-blade wooden propeller (many different propeller installations were tried) at a low rpm. The exhaust was carefully muffled. The Q-Star led to the fully-military Lockheed YO-3A developed during 1968-69.

208. The YO-3A was based upon the Schweizer SGS-232. An advanced technology six-bladed propeller was mated to a six-cylinder Continental engine while a long muffler and exhaust ran the entire length of the fuselage to dampen noise and reduce infrared emissions. They had a crew of two. The YO-3As were operated over sensitive areas, in Vietnam, but were apparently a complete failure.

209. Beech QU-22Bs (69-7693 through 69-7705, 70-1535 through 70-1548) were deployed in South Vietnam in the IGLOO WHITE mission laying down and receiving data from ADSIDS. They were to replace the obsolete Lockheed EC-121R Constellations that were performing the data link portion of the mission, but, apparently operating under the control of the 553rd Reconnaissance Wing, the QU-22Bs appear not to have functioned in the drone (Q) role, being manually operated by a pilot and systems operator, and operational results were so disappointing that the EC-121Rs were retained and some of the QU-22Bs attached to the FAC role. The QU-22B did not make the best FAC aircraft and after several were shot down the type was withdrawn from service.

210. The North American OV-10A Bronco was created to fill the military's requirement for a counterinsurgency (COIN) aircraft to use in Southeast Asia. First flown in August 1967, it was acquired by the USAF, USN and USMC for use in the FAC role and for limited quick-response ground support until heavier, more specialized attack aircraft could arrive. Production stopped in April 1969. The USAF received 157 OV-10A.

209

9

BLANDFORD WAR PHOTO-FILES

THE MODERN ERA

211. Lockheed S-3A Viking of Air Anti-Submarine Squadron Thirty-Seven (VS-37) on the flight deck of the USS *Constellation* (CV-64) on 13 December 1978. The Viking came about as a replacement for the Tracker through the need to provide the Fleet with more advanced ASW aircraft. The first YS-3A flew on 21 January 1972 from Palmdale, California. The S-3A entered service with VS-41 during February 1974 at North Island, California.

Powered by two General Electric TF34-GE-2 turbofans, it spans 68 ft 8 in (29 ft 6 in folded), is 53 ft 4 in long and 22 ft 9 in high, and has a 518 mph top speed and normal range of 2000 miles. They are equipped with the Univac AN/AYK-10 digital computer, Texas Instruments AN/APS-116 radar in the nose, Texas Instruments OR-89 FLIR (Forward Looking Infra-Red) scanner in a retractable ventral radome, AN/ASQ-81 MAD

(Magnetic Anomaly Detector) sensor, an IBM AN/ALR-47 ECM system and 60 sonobuoys. The bomb bay can carry 2000 lb of offensive weapons and underwing hard points can carry Harpoons, bombs, rockets or fuel tanks. A total of 187 S-3A Vikings was built. Two S-3B prototypes have been tested with a view to converting surviving S-3A.

212

212. Its MAD boom fully deployed, an S-3A begins to overfly a surfaced submarine during military exercises.

213. Grumman E-2C Hawkeye moving into position for a catapult launching from the nuclear-powered USS *Nimitz* (CVN-68) in January 1980 during training in the Indian Ocean.

214. The E-2C is the latest version of the US Navy's very advanced carrier-operated AEW control platform. E-2As became operational during 1965. The E-2C represents a significant advance in electronics over the E-2A. The first flew on 20 January 1971 and entered operational service in late 1973. Powered by two Allison T56-A-452 turboprops, it has an 80 ft 7 in span, 57 ft 7 in length, 52,000 lb maximum take-off weight and 374 mph top speed. A crew of five or six can be carried on six-hour missions, during which the E-2C can scan targets anywhere within three million cubic miles. It is also operated by Japan and Israel. Although the prime mission is detecting and locating hostile aircraft, it also serves as a command and control station. Advanced electronics allow its three operators to monitor and control hundreds of aircraft.

213

214

215. One of the two E-2C Hawkeyes from VAW-125 used during the second launching of the Space Shuttle *Columbia* in November 1981. Positioned at 24,000 ft and 75 miles north of the launch site, they used their aerial command post capability to monitor air traffic by coordinating with the Kennedy Space Center's range officer via real-time data link. The Hawkeyes tracked 20 NASA and military aircraft that operated in the air space during the launch while preventing any unauthorized aircraft from entering the range. Once the *Columbia's* reusable booster rockets separated from the Shuttle, the Hawkeyes directed four recovery ships stationed offshore to the splashdown site for the recovery of the units. The large rotodome atop the fuselage houses General Electric AN/APS-125 search radar. Used with the AN/APA-171 antenna group, the system can detect small objects such as cruise missiles at up to 115 miles while large objects can be detected up to 300 miles from the E-2C. A new antenna for the rotodome has been tested to upgrade the aircraft's passive detection system in order to pick up unusual emitters and provide automatic triangulation location.

215

216. Sikorsky SH-3D Sea King from Helicopter Anti-submarine Squadron Two (HS-2) drops a parachute retarded torpedo into San Diego Bay, California, during a practice attack on 22 December 1975. The US Navy has always stressed the importance of ASW aircraft and helicopters to keep the Fleet as protected from the deadly menace as possible. Designed in 1957 to meet a USN ASW requirement, the basic H-3 has been adopted for a wide variety of roles and has been sold to many foreign countries. The Sea King's specialized equipment for ASW operations includes active / passive dipping sonar, active / passive sonobuoys, MAD gear, automatic stabilization equipment and surface search radar, and weapons include nuclear torpedoes and up to four Mk 46 torpedoes. The SH-3D is an upgraded variant of the SH-3A with two 1400 hp T58-GE-10 turboshafts; 74 were constructed for the Navy's anti-submarine squadrons. It carries two pilots and two sonar operators, and has a cruise of 136 mph and range of 625 miles.

217. A Sikorsky SH-3A Sea King lowering a sonar dome during an anti-submarine warfare training exercise, while flying from the ASW carrier USS *Hornet* (CVS-12) on 24 January 1969.

218 The Sikorsky EH-60A Quick Fix helicopter is one of the US Army's new Special Electronics Mission Aircraft (SEMA) and is a derivative of the UH-60A Black Hawk utility transport. The basic Black Hawk configuration has been modified to accommodate an 1800 lb electronics package which includes four dipole antennae mounted on the rear of the fuselage and a deployable whip antenna mounted underneath the fuselage. The Quick Fix's mission is intercepting, monitoring and jamming enemy radio communications signals. The EH-60A is powered by two General Electric T700-GE700 turboshaft engines rated at 1560 shp each, giving a cruise speed of 138 knots.

219. Sikorsky's SH-60B Seahawk is a high-performance helicopter that also utilizes the technology of the UH-60A Black Hawk tactical transport. The Seahawk is designed to perform a primary mission of anti-submarine warfare (ASW) and anti-ship surveillance and targeting (ASST) utilizing standard internal fuel. In addition, the helicopter can perform secondary missions of SAR, medevac and vertical replenishment.

218

219

220. Grumman's superlative F-14A Tomcat heavy fighter now has added capabilities courtesy of the Tactical Air Reconnaissance Pod System (TARPS) suspended between the engines. Designed for a low to medium altitude clear-air-mass reconnaissance role, the pod contains a KS-87 frame camera, a KA-99 panoramic camera and an AAD-5 infrared line scanner. The F-14 is modified to accommodate pod operation controls in the naval flight officer's cockpit (second seat) and to provide electrical power and air conditioning to the pod. The TARPS has been assigned to selected F-14 squadrons, deployment having begun in 1981. Air and ground crew training takes place at Miramar NAS, California, and Oceana NAS, Virginia.

221. This image recorded by Goodyear Aerospace radar from extremely high altitude, shows London, the Thames and the English Channel in very sharp detail. Ships appear as white spots on the black sea. The white line jutting south into the river near the center is a pier almost a mile and a half long. Not only of strategic importance, such images can be used for civic planning and resources management.

220

221

222. With the reconnaissance ability of the Fleet greatly reduced by the withdrawal of the effective RF-8 Crusader, the Navy has been searching for a practical answer to the requirement for a dedicated photo-recon mount. The answer once again appears to be a converted fighter—the McDonnell Douglas RF/A-18 Hornet. The first 'RF' variant is seen in flight, banking to show off the camera and sensor bays mounted in the new forward fuselage. This version of the Hornet can also defend itself since most of the armament of the fighter/attack variant is retained.

223. The Northrop Corporation's rugged F-5 series of tactical fighters have found customers in many parts of the world. In 1983, the company developed the RF-5E TigerEye, a reconnaissance version of the combat aircraft. The RF-5E has a completely redesigned forward fuselage section to accommodate a wide variety of sensor equipment capable of performing missions around-the-clock, from low altitudes up to 50,000 ft. The all-black company-owned demonstrator is seen at the Palmdale, California, assembly plant.

224. 1984 saw the appearance in European skies of operational Grumman/General Dynamics EF-111A Raven Electronic Warfare aircraft. A conversion of the basic F-111A airframe, the Raven has been fitted with as many 'off the shelf' black boxes as possible in order to speed introduction into service and keep costs down. Designed for carrying out important defense suppression missions in support of the USAF's Tactical Air Command, the Raven carries a very powerful ALQ-99E primary jammer which lets the aircraft penetrate the densest known enemy electronic defenses. The crew capsule of the Raven has been revised while the new vertical tail carries the ALQ-99E receivers. Studies are already underway for increasing the Raven's jamming capability in view of rapidly increasing Soviet threats. The first operational EF-111A unit is the 390th Electronic Combat Squadron at Mountain Home AFB, Idaho, while the second unit is the 42nd ECS at RAF Upper Heyford. Forty-two Ravens are being converted by Grumman from early F-111A airframes.

223

224

225. The Lockheed P-3 Airborne Early Warning and Control (AEW&C) prototype first flew during 1984, having been converted from a surplus Royal Australian Air Force Orion. The large rotodome mounts the antenna for the General Electric APS 138 radar, giving the Orion the capability to patrol, survey, detect and track enemy air and surface traffic while acting as a command center for friendly counterforces. A similar conversion is also planned for the company's Hercules transport. The modification, according to Lockheed, would give the prospective purchaser the radius of action and time on station comparable to the Boeing E-3A but at less than half the price.

226. This Lockheed C-141A StarLifter transport, s/n 61-2777, was the subject of an interesting modification. The entire rear fuselage, from the rear loading doors back, was reconfigured by the 4950th Test Wing Modification Center, Wright Patterson AFB, to carry directive infrared countermeasures equipment. This project tested equipment that could detect and confuse infrared heat seeking anti-aircraft missiles.

225

227. The EC-135N, with its huge drooped radar nose, is immediately identifiable. These aircraft, usually based out of Patrick AFB, Florida, were extensively used during the Apollo spaceflight program for tracking missile shots and the re-entry of spacecraft. The markings on the fuselage side of the first aircraft are for photometric purposes.

228. EC-135P modified for the AFSATCOM (Air Force Satellite Communications System) mission. Constantly modified to reflect changing technology, these command, control and communications (C^3) aircraft usually sport odd radomes and antennae. The streamlined radome atop is for an omni-directional antenna. EC-135Ps are real-time linked to SAC headquarters, various airfields and commands and SAC missile silos.

227

228

229. Surely one of the most imposing aircraft in this volume, the massive Boeing E-4B Airborne Command Post is based on the commercial 747 airliner. Initially, three E-4As were built to support the National Emergency Airborne Command Post (NEACP) mission and interfaced with existing Boeing EC-135 Command Control and Communications (C^3) equipment. Four fully-developed E-4B Airborne Command Post aircraft (three converted from the E-4As) are in the process of completely taking over the NEACP mission. The E-4Bs have been hardened against the effects of nuclear explosions, have a powerful 1200kVA electrical system to support advanced electronics, provision for inflight refuelling and new communications equipment including direct satellite link. They are based with SAC at Offutt AFB, Nebraska.

230. The Boeing C-135—one aircraft whose many sky spy modifications and variants could fill this entire volume—is based on the successful transport/tanker. Boeing built 808. Many have been repeatedly modified for clandestine duties. This KC-135A, with refuelling gear removed, was fitted with telemetry relay gear for operations with the USAF's airborne laser lab (another modified C-135).

229

BIBLIOGRAPHY

Babington-Smith, Constance, *Evidence In Camera*, Chatto and Windus, London, 1958
Bell, Dana, *Air Force Colors* Vol. 1 1926-42 and Vol. 2 1942-45, Squadron / Signal, Carrollton, Texas
Bowers, Peter, *Curtiss Aircraft 1907-1947*, Putnam, London, 1979
Brookes, Andrew J., *Photo Reconnaissance*, Ian Allen, England, 1975
Francillon, Rene J., *McDonnell Douglas Aircraft Since 1920*, Putnam, London, 1979
Francillon, Rene J., *Lockheed Aircraft Since 1913*, Putnam, London, 1982

Freeman, Roger A., *Camouflage and Markings USAAF 1937-1945*, Ducimus, London, 1974
Gunston, Bill, *Spy Planes*, Salamander, London, 1983
Hirst, Mike, *Airborne Early Warning*, Osprey, London, 1983
Infield, Glenn B., *Unarmed and Unafraid*, Macmillan, New York, 1970
Miller, Jay, *Lockheed U-2*, Aerofax, Austin, Texas, 1983
Miller, Jay, *Lockheed SR-71*, Aerofax, Austin, Texas, 1983

Streetly, Martin, *World Electronic Warfare Aircraft*, Jane's, London, 1983
Swanborough, Gordon and Bowers, Peter M., *United States Navy Aircraft Since 1911*, Putnam, London, 1976
Swanborough, Gordon and Bowers, Peter M., *United States Military Aircraft Since 1911*, Putnam, 1963
Wagner, Ray, *American Combat Planes*, Doubleday, New York, 1977
White, William, *The Little Toy Dog*, E.P. Dutton, New York, 1962

INDEX